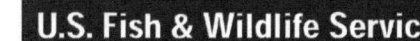
U.S. Fish & Wildlife Service

Comprehensive Conservation Plan

Block Island National Wildlife Refuge

Prepared by:

Nancy McGarigal, Refuge Planner
Northeast Regional Office, Division of Planning
300 Westgate Center Drive
Hadley, MA 01035
(413) 253-8562

Local contact:

Charlie Vandemoer, Refuge Manager
3769 D Old Post Road
Charlestown, RI 02813
(401) 364-9124

Cover photo: American burying beetle, Chris Raithel, RI DEM

May 2002

This goose, designed by J.N. `Ding" Darling, has become a symbol of the National Wildlife Refuge System.

The *U.S. Fish & Wildlife Service* is the principal federal agency responsible for conserving, protecting, and enhancing fish and wildlife and their habitats for the continuing benefit of the American people. The Service manages the 93-million acre National Wildlife Refuge System comprised of more than 500 national wildlife refuges and thousands of waterfowl production areas. It also operates 66 national fish hatcheries and 78 ecological services field stations. The agency enforces federal wildlife laws, manages migratory bird populations, restores nationally significant fisheries, conserves and restores wildlife habitat such as wetlands, administers the Endangered Species Act, and helps foreign governments with their conservation efforts. It also oversees the Federal Aid program which distributes hundreds of millions of dollars in excise taxes on fishing and hunting equipment to state wildlife agencies.

Comprehensive Conservation Plans provide long term guidance for management decisions; set forth goals, objectives, and strategies needed to accomplish refuge purposes; and, identify the Service's best estimate of future needs. These plans detail program planning levels that are sometimes substantially above current budget allocations and, as such, are primarily for Service strategic planning and program prioritization purposes. The plans do not constitute a commitment for staffing increases, operational and maintenance increases, or funding for future land acquisition.

Comprehensive Conservation Plan Approval
for Block Island National Wildlife Refuge

Submitted by:

Charles E. Vandemoer,
Refuge Manager,
Rhode Island NWR Complex

6/21/02
Date

Approved by:

Richard W. Dyer,
Refuge Supervisor, North
National Wildlife Refuge System

7/16/02
Date

Approved by:

Anthony D. Léger,
Northeast Regional Chief,
National Wildlife Refuge System

8/9/02
Date

Final approval:

Dr. Mamie A. Parker,
Regional Director, Region 5
U.S. Fish and Wildlife Service

8/13/02
Date

Table of Contents

Block Island National Wildlife Refuge CCP

Chapter 1

North Light on Block Island
USFWS photo

Introduction and Background

- Refuge Overview
- Purpose of and Need for a CCP
- Mission
- Refuge Purpose
- National and Regional Mandates Guiding this CCP
- Existing Partnerships

Introduction

This Comprehensive Conservation Plan (CCP) is the culmination of a planning process that began in February 1998. Numerous meetings with the public, the state, and conservation partners were held to identify and evaluate management alternatives. A draft Comprehensive Conservation Plan and Environmental Assessment (CCP/EA) was distributed in December 2000. This CCP presents the management goals, objectives, and strategies that we believe will best achieve our vision for the refuge, contribute to the National Wildlife Refuge System Mission, achieve refuge purposes and legal mandates, and serve the American public.

Refuge Overview

Established in 1973, Block Island National Wildlife Refuge (Block Island Refuge) is located approximately 12 miles off the mainland on Block Island, Town of New Shoreham (see maps 1-1 and 1-2). The transfer of 28.7 acres from the U.S. Coast Guard created the refuge. The refuge now includes 103 acres in either fee title or conservation easement. The Land Protection Plan (Appendix E) expanded the refuge acquisition boundary by 95 acres; the refuge may now acquire a total of 156 acres from willing sellers within the newly expanded boundary.

Thirty percent of Block Island is currently in conservation status, including lands owned or administered by the Service, The Nature Conservancy, Block Island Land Trust, Block Island Conservancy, Town of New Shoreham, Audubon Society of Rhode Island, and individual private land owners. In 1989, New Shoreham passed a referendum that transfers 3 percent of property taxes into a land acquisition fund administered by the Block Island Land Trust.

The Purpose of and Need for a CCP

Developing a CCP is vital to refuge management. The purpose of this CCP is to provide strategic management direction over the next 15 years, by...

- Providing a clear statement of desired future conditions for habitat, wildlife, visitor services, and facilities;
- Providing refuge neighbors, visitors, and partners with a clear understanding of the reasons for management actions;
- Ensuring refuge management reflects the policies and goals of the Refuge System and legal mandates;
- Ensuring the compatibility of current and future public use;
- Providing long-term continuity and direction for refuge management; and
- Providing direction for staffing, operations, maintenance, and developing budget requests.

The need to develop a CCP for Block Island Refuge is two-fold. First, the 1997 National Wildlife Refuge System Improvement Act (Refuge Improvement Act) requires that all national wildlife refuges have a CCP in place by 2012 to help fulfill the mission of the Refuge

Map 1-1

Rhode Island National Wildlife Refuge Complex
U.S. Fish & Wildlife Service Current Ownership

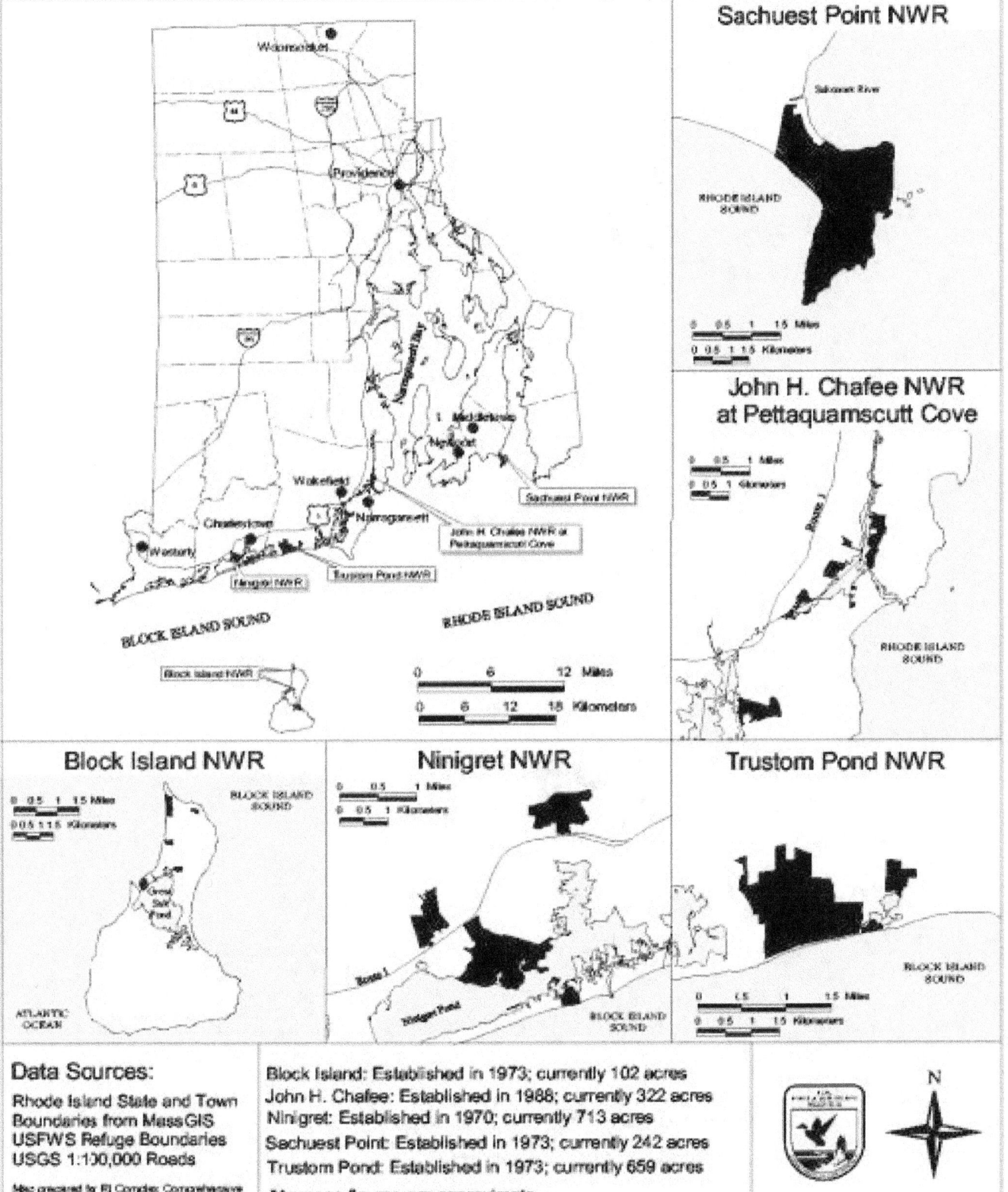

Sachuest Point NWR

John H. Chafee NWR at Pettaquamscutt Cove

Block Island NWR

Ninigret NWR

Trustom Pond NWR

Data Sources:

Rhode Island State and Town
Boundaries from MassGIS
USFWS Refuge Boundaries
USGS 1:100,000 Roads

Map prepared for RI Complex Comprehensive
Conservation Plan, March 2002

Block Island: Established in 1973; currently 102 acres
John H. Chafee: Established in 1988; currently 322 acres
Ninigret: Established in 1970; currently 713 acres
Sachuest Point: Established in 1973; currently 242 acres
Trustom Pond: Established in 1973; currently 659 acres

*Acreage figures are approximate.

N

Map 1-2

Block Island National Wildlife Refuge
Current Ownership and Approved Acquisition Boundary
Rhode Island NWR Complex Comprehensive Conservation Plan

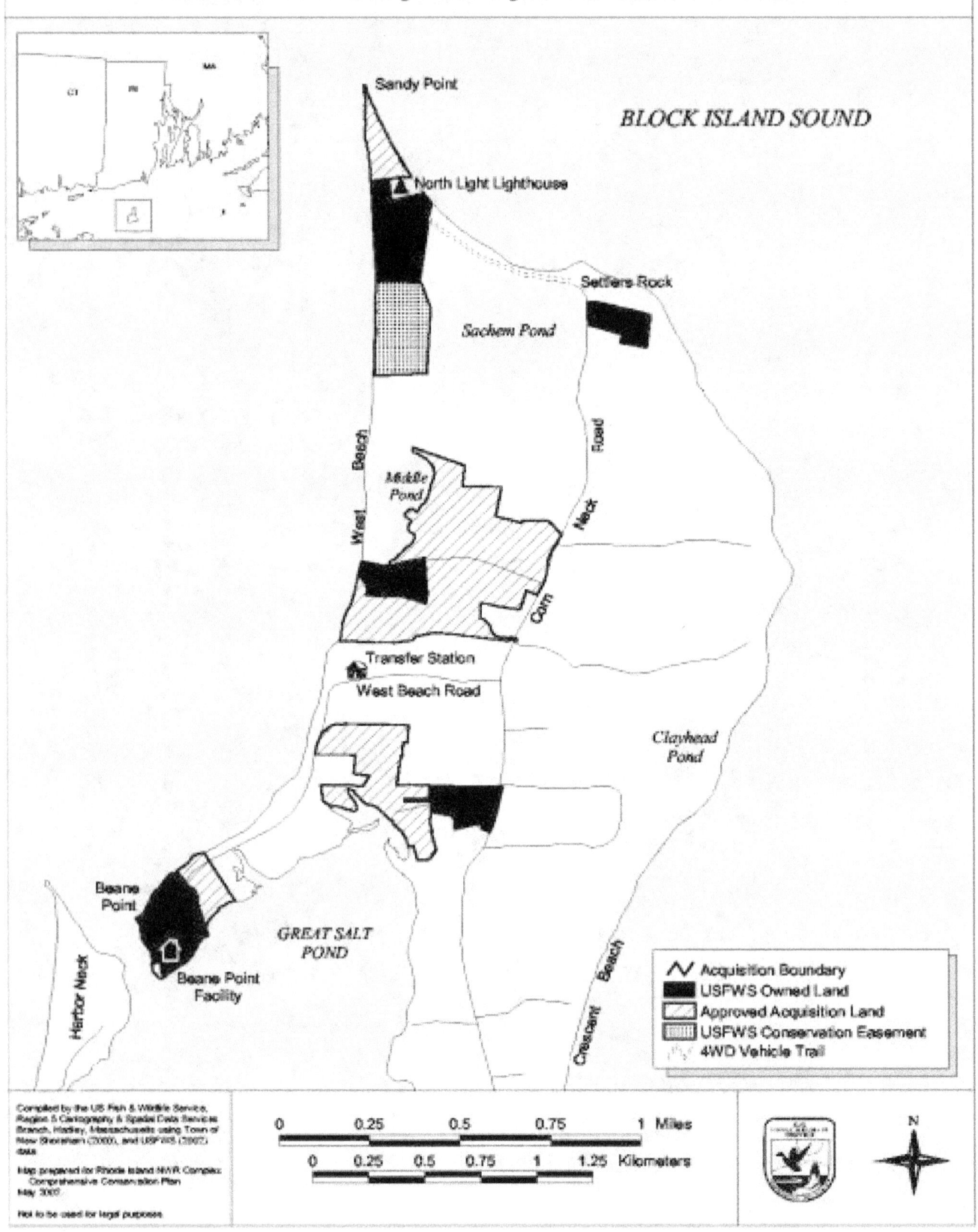

System. Second, the refuge lacks a master plan that establishes priorities and ensures consistent, integrated management among the five refuges in the Rhode Island Refuge Complex.

The U.S. Fish and Wildlife Service and its Mission

The Service, part of the Department of the Interior, manages national wildlife refuges and national fish hatcheries. By law, Congress entrusts the following federal trust resources to the Service for conservation and protection: migratory birds and fish, endangered species, inter-jurisdictional fish, wetlands, and certain marine mammals. The Service also enforces federal wildlife laws and international treaties on importing and exporting wildlife, assists with state fish and wildlife programs, and helps other countries develop wildlife conservation programs.

The National Wildlife Refuge System and its Mission

The Refuge System is the world's largest collection of lands and waters set aside specifically for conserving wildlife and protecting ecosystems. More than 534 national wildlife refuges, in every state and a number of U.S. Territories, protect more than 93 million acres. Over 34 million visitors annually hunt, fish, observe and photograph wildlife, or participate in environmental education and interpretive activities on refuges.

In 1997, Congress passed the National Wildlife Refuge System Improvement Act, establishing a unifying mission for the Refuge System, and a new process for determining compatible public use activities on refuges. It also requires that we prepare a CCP for each refuge. The act states that, first and foremost, the Refuge System must focus on wildlife conservation. It further states that the mission of the Refuge System, coupled with the purpose(s) for which each refuge was established, will provide management direction for each refuge.

On public use, the act declares that all existing or proposed public uses must be compatible with each refuge's purpose. It highlights six wildlife-dependent public uses as priorities that all CCPs must evaluate: environmental education and interpretation, fishing, hunting, and wildlife observation and photography. Each refuge manager determines the compatibility of an activity by evaluating its potential impact on refuge resources, insuring that the activity supports the Refuge System mission, and ensuring that the activity does not materially detract from or interfere with the refuge purpose.

Refuge Purpose

The establishment purposes for Block Island Refuge are:

"... for use as an inviolate sanctuary, or for any other management purpose, for migratory birds," and for

"(1) incidental fish and wildlife oriented recreational development;
(2) protection of natural resources; and
(3) conservation of endangered or threatened species."

– Migratory Bird Conservation Act of 1929 and
Refuge Recreation Act of 1962

"...working with others, to conserve, protect and enhance fish wildlife, and plants and their habitats for the continuing benefit of the American people."

– Mission, U.S. Fish &
Wildlife Service

"...to administer a national network of lands and waters for the conservation, management, and where appropriate, restoration of the fish, wildlife, and plant resources and their habitats within the United States for the benefit of present and future generations of Americans."

– Refuge System Mission,
Refuge Improvement Act;
Public Law 105-57

National and Regional Mandates Guiding this CCP

This section highlights Service policy, legal mandates, and existing resource plans, arranged from the national to the local level, that directly influenced development of this CCP.

The *Digest of Federal Resource Laws of Interest to the USFWS* lists the various federal laws, Executive Orders, treaties, interstate compacts, and regulations on conserving and protecting natural and cultural resources (online at http://laws.fws.gov/lawsdigest/indx.html). The Service Manual and Refuge Manual contain Service policies and guidance on planning and day-to-day refuge management. The draft CCP/EA was written to fulfill compliance with the National Environmental Policy Act (NEPA).

North American Waterfowl Management Plan (May 14, 1986)

Black duck. *USFWS photo.*

This plan outlines the strategy among the United States, Canada, and Mexico to restore waterfowl populations by protecting, restoring, and enhancing habitat within 11 U.S. Joint Venture Areas and three species Joint Ventures: Arctic Goose, Black Duck, and Sea Duck. Partnerships among federal, state and provincial governments, tribal nations, local businesses, conservation organizations, and individual citizens protect that habitat. The Refuge Complex lies within the Atlantic Coast Joint Venture, which has identified 13 priority focus areas totaling 3,226 acres of both wetlands and adjacent uplands for protection in Rhode Island (Atlantic Coast Joint Venture 1988).

Since black ducks winter in Rhode Island, the goals and objectives of the Black Duck Joint Venture apply to managing the Refuge Complex. The Black Duck Joint Venture has identified the coastal salt marsh habitats along the mid-upper Atlantic coast as most important wintering habitat.

Partners in Flight Landbird Conservation Plan: Physiographic Area 9, Southern New England (draft, October 2000)

In 1990, Partners in Flight (PIF) was conceived as a voluntary, international coalition of government agencies, conservation organizations, academic institutions, private industry, and other citizens dedicated to reversing the downward trends of declining species and "keeping common birds common." The foundation of PIF's long-term strategy for bird conservation is a series of scientifically based Landbird Conservation Plans. The goal of each PIF Landbird Conservation Plan is to ensure long term maintenance of healthy populations of native landbirds.

The PIF Program is developing a plan for the Southern New England Physiographic Area, using existing data on habitat loss, landbird population trends, and the vulnerability of species and habitats to threats, to rank the conservation priority of landbird species. The plan will identify focal species for each habitat type from which population and habitat objectives and conservation actions will be determined. We utilized this draft document for the list of priority species to consider in management. A revised draft of the plan was released in October 2000, and we will use the final plan, when finished, to further guide management.

Northeast Areas Study: Significant Coastal Habitats of Southern New England And Portions of Long Island, New York (USFWS 1991)

Recognizing the biological and economic importance of the coast's living resources and natural values to the region and the Nation, in 1990 Congress funded a study to identify coastal areas in southern New England and Long Island whose fish and wildlife habitat need protection and whose natural diversity needs preservation. The Northeast Coastal Study identifies species of regional importance, and describes regionally significant habitat complexes. It specifically describes significant or unique habitat, threats to sustaining the habitat complex, and considerations for conserving and protecting it. We utilized this study in the development of our land protection strategies. The study identified Block Island as a regionally significant habitat complex.

Connecticut River/Long Island Sound Ecosystem Priorities, 1997

During the last decade, we have emphasized ecosystem conservation, particularly the role of refuges within ecosystems, and their ability to affect the long-term conservation of natural resources. Implementing an ecosystem approach to resource management is one of our top national priorities. We have initiated new partnerships with private landowners, state and federal agencies, corporations, conservation groups, and volunteers, to form 52 ecosystem teams across the country, typically using large river watersheds to define ecosystems. Those teams work on developing goals and priorities for research and management within each ecosystem.

The Refuge Complex lies within our Connecticut River/Long Island Sound Ecosystem (Map 1-3). A team composed of Fish and Wildlife Service personnel and representatives from six State Fish and Wildlife Departments developed a Priority Resources Plan (July 1996) that identifies seven priorities, each involving numerous action strategies.

1. Protect, restore, and enhance listed and candidate populations...with special emphasis on beach strand species, coastal sandplain habitat, and Connecticut River species.

2. Protect, restore, and enhance anadromous and interjurisdictional migratory fish populations...with special emphasis on Atlantic salmon, American shad, shortnose sturgeon, and river herring.

3. Reverse the decline of migrant landbirds...with special emphasis on grassland and forest interior species.

4. Protect, restore, and enhance populations of colonial nesting waterbirds, shorebirds, and waterfowl...with special emphasis on coastal areas and major rivers.

5. Protect, restore, and enhance wetland habitats.

6. Manage refuge lands to protect, restore, and enhance native communities and trust resources.

7. Develop a public that values the fish and wildlife resources...understands events and issues related to these resources, and acts to promote fish and wildlife conservation.

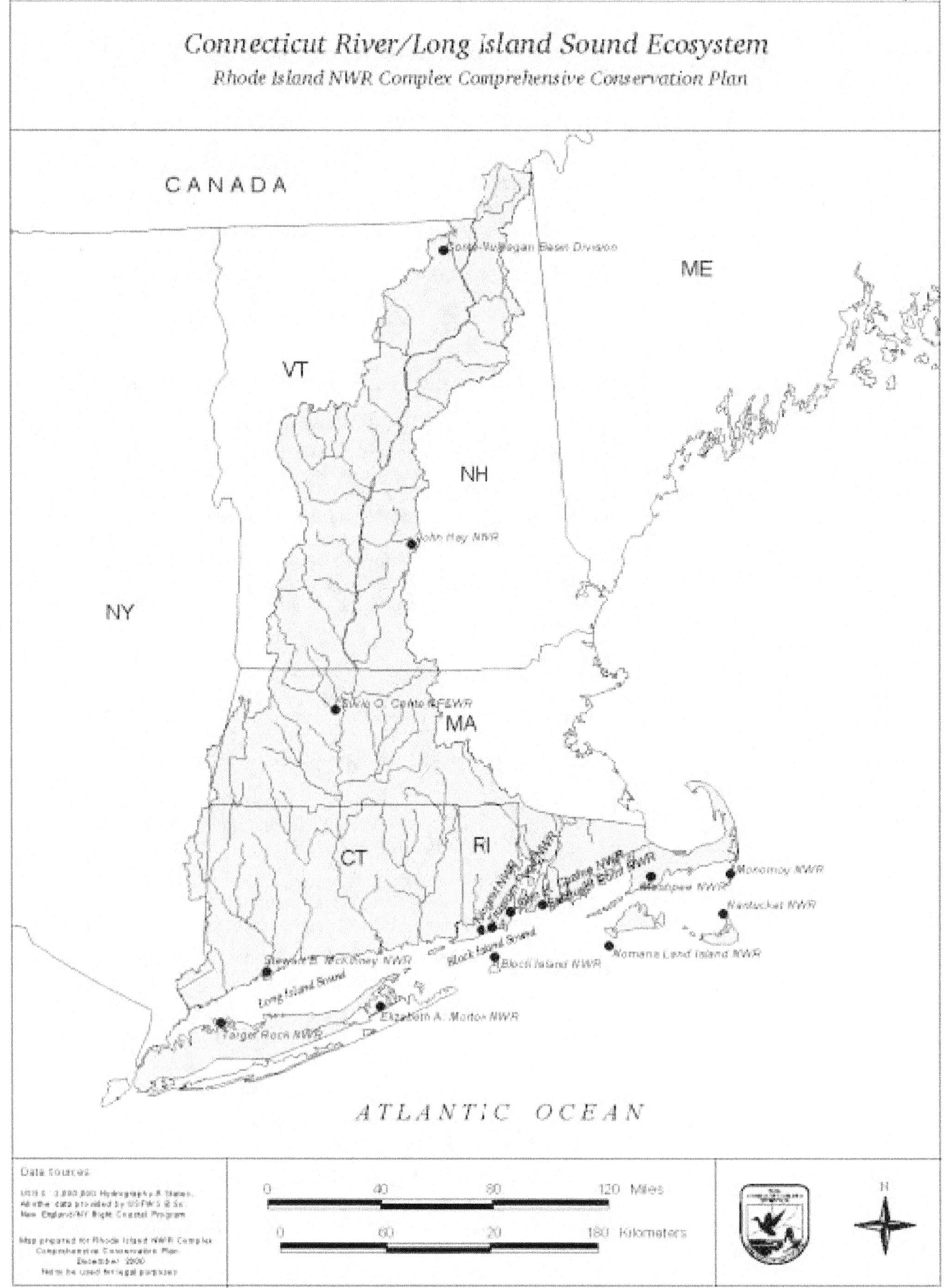

Connecticut River/Long Island Sound Ecosystem
Rhode Island NWR Complex Comprehensive Conservation Plan

CANADA

ME

VT

NH

NY

MA

CT

RI

ATLANTIC OCEAN

Piping Plover (*Charadrius melodus*), Atlantic Coast Population, Revised Recovery Plan, 1996

Piping plover. *USFWS photo.*

The piping plover is the only federally-listed endangered or threatened species that currently breeds on refuge lands within the Rhode Island Refuge Complex. In 2001 on Block Island, piping plover nested on a contiguous stretch of beach immediately adjacent to the refuge. The primary objective of the revised recovery program is to remove the Atlantic coast piping plover population from the List of Endangered and Threatened Wildlife and Plants by:

- Achieving well-distributed increases in numbers and productivity of breeding pairs; and
- Providing for long-term protection of breeding and wintering plovers and their habitats.

The Revised Recovery Plan describes detailed "Recovery Tasks" needed to meet the recovery objective. The Rhode Island Refuge Complex is specifically mentioned in the following tasks:

- Draw down or create coastal ponds where feasible to make more feeding habitat available.
- Reduce disturbance of breeding plovers from humans and pets.
- Develop mechanisms to provide long-term protection of plovers and their habitat.

The Recovery Plan incorporates management guidelines for recreational activities in piping plover breeding habitat, which were developed by our Ecological Services Division in 1994. While not regulatory, these recommendations continue to serve as our best professional advice for complying with the Endangered Species Act. We utilized these same guidelines in developing management actions.

American Burying Beetle (*Nicrophorus americanus*) Recovery Plan, 1991

The American burying beetle is a federally endangered species that is known to breed on southern Block Island, but no breeding behavior has yet been observed on Block Island Refuge. One female was recorded on the Beane tract, but was not seen on subsequent visits. No extensive surveys have been conducted on the refuge; interest has focused on southern Block Island, where the core population is assumed to breed. Since the island supports the only known natural population east of the Mississippi River, any opportunity to protect or enhance habitat for this species is a priority.

The Recovery Plan objective is "…[to] reduce the immediacy of the threat of extinction to the American burying beetle, and the longer range objective is to improve its status so that it can be reclassified from endangered to threatened." It outlines nine specific Recovery Tasks for managing the existing populations, searching for new populations, re-introducing populations, conducting natural history studies, and starting an environmental education program.

Regional Wetlands Concept Plan – Emergency Wetlands Resources Act 9 (USFWS 1990)

In 1986, Congress enacted the Emergency Wetlands Resources Act to promote the conservation of our nation's wetlands. The Act directed the Department of Interior to develop a National Wetlands Priority Conservation Plan identifying the location and types of wetlands that should receive priority for acquisition by federal and state agencies using Land and Water Conservation Fund appropriations. In 1990, the Service's Northeast Region completed a Regional Wetlands Concept Plan identifying a total of 850 wetland sites in the Region warranting consideration for acquisition due to wetland values. Wetland values, functions, and potential threats for each site were cited; 24 sites within the State of Rhode Island were listed.

Protecting Our Land Resources:
A Land Acquisition and Protection Plan, Rhode Island Department of Environmental Management, May 1996

The purpose of this State plan is to assist agencies within the Rhode Island Department of Environmental Management (RI DEM) in protecting land to support their primary mission, "...protection of the integrity of natural resources essential to the environmental, economic and social welfare of the citizens of Rhode Island." Its framework provides strategies to permanently protect five critical State resources: agriculture, forestry, drinking water, recreation, and natural heritage and biodiversity. It includes evaluation criteria for selecting and prioritizing lands.

Existing partnerships

Throughout this CCP, we use the term "partners". In addition to our volunteers, we receive significant help from the following partners:

- Southern New England/New York Bight Coastal Ecosystems Office (FWS)
- Ecological Services, New England Field Office (FWS)
- Friends of the National Wildlife Refuges of Rhode Island
- Rhode Island Department of Environmental Management (RI DEM)
- The Nature Conservancy, Rhode Island and Block Island Offices
- University of Rhode Island, Department of Natural Resources Science (URI)
- Audubon Society of Rhode Island
- Rhode Island Coastal Resources Management Council (RI CRMC)
- Local land trusts
- Narragansett Indian Tribal Council
- Town of New Shoreham
- Block Island Conservancy

Chapter 2

Public Open House on CCP, Rhode Island
USFWS photo

Planning Process

- The Comprehensive Conservation Planning Process
- Issues, Concerns, and Opportunities

The Comprehensive Conservation Planning Process

Given the mandate in the Refuge Improvement Act to develop a CCP for each national wildlife refuge, our Northeast Regional Office began the planning process for the Refuge Complex in February 1998. Figure 2-1 displays the steps of the planning process and how they incorporate National Environmental Policy Act (NEPA) requirements.

First, we focused on collecting information on natural resources and public use at the Refuge Complex, and developed its long-term vision and preliminary goals, including issues associated with each of its refuges. Next, we compiled a mailing list of more than 2,000 organizations and individuals, to ensure we would be contacting a diverse sample of the interested public.

Recognizing that not everyone could attend the open houses planned for April and May 1998, we developed Issues Workbooks in March, to encourage even more people to provide their written comments on topics related to managing the Refuge Complex. We offered the workbooks to everyone on our mailing list, including adjacent landowners, and made workbooks available at refuge headquarters, local libraries, and on the Internet from the Region 5 Home Page (http://www.northeast.fws.gov). We received 150 completed workbooks. Those responses and public input at our meetings have influenced our formulating issues and developing alternatives on resource protection and public use.

Figure 2-1. *NEPA and the CCP Process*

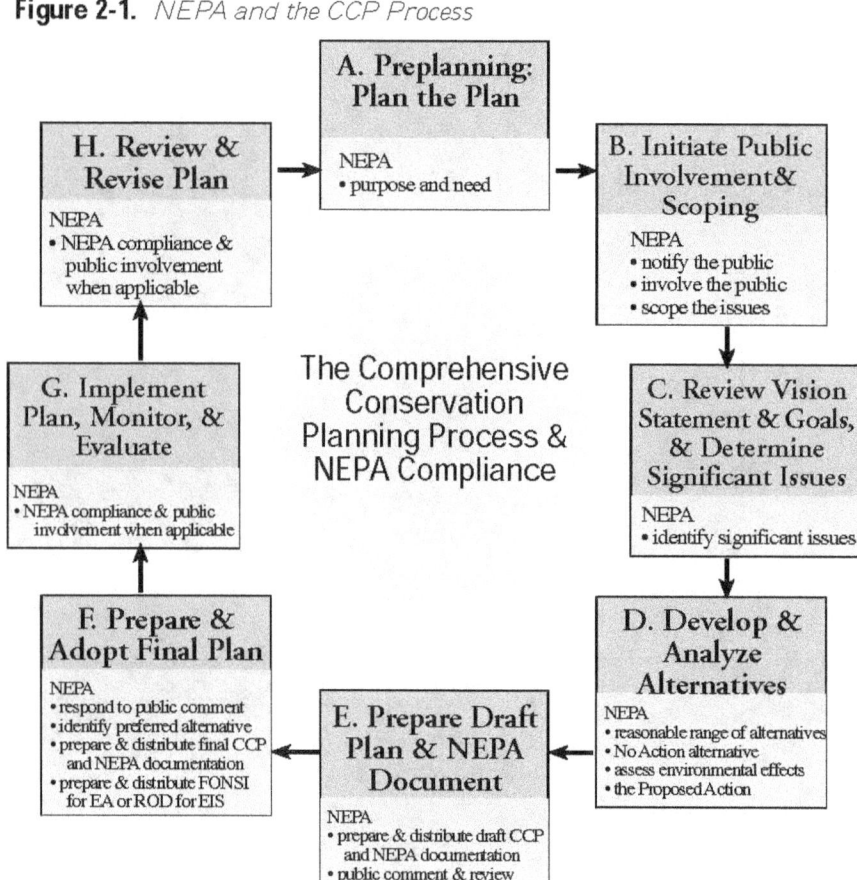

In April and May 1998, we began a series of public meetings: five open houses in the communities of Middletown, South Kingstown, Charlestown, and Block Island invited public comments on goals and issues. We advertised the meetings through news releases, radio broadcasts, and notices to our mailing list. From 15 to 40 people attended each meeting. We also organized 15 informational meetings with state and federal agencies, non-profit conservation groups, town planners, conservation commissions, and sporting clubs.

Public responses suggested more than 50 additional areas where lands warranted protection, typically along the coast. We evaluated those lands for their potential as national wildlife refuges, using criteria such as the presence of threatened, endangered, or other trust species and their habitats, the presence of wetlands, our ability to manage or restore the areas, existing threats to their integrity, and their size and location.

We distributed a planning update to everyone on our mailing list in September 1998. This newsletter summarized public comments from meetings and workbooks, described policy guidelines for managing public use on refuges, and identified the long-term vision and goals for the Refuge Complex.

Once the key issues had firmed up, we developed alternative strategies by May 1999 to resolve each one. We derived the strategies from public comment, from follow-up contacts with partners, or from the planning team. We distributed a second Planning Update newsletter in May 1999, updating everyone on our planning timelines and our decision to start a separate Environmental Assessment for the visitor center/headquarters.

We released a draft CCP/EA in December of 2000 for a 51-day comment period. We held public hearings and open houses in February of 2001. A summary of public comments is included in Appendix B. The land acquisition component of this planning process is contained in the Land Protection Plan (Appendix E).

Each year, we will evaluate our accomplishments under this CCP, including the completion of detailed step down plans. Monitoring will reveal whether resource objectives are being met, and whether we need to change strategies. We will modify the CCP documents and associated management activities as needed, following the procedures outlined in Service policy and NEPA requirements. This CCP will be fully revised every 15 years, or sooner if necessary.

Issues, Concerns, and Opportunities

From the Issues Workbooks, public and focus group meetings, and planning team discussions, we developed a list of issues, concerns, opportunities, or any other items requiring a management decision. Then we sorted them into two categories: "Key issues," and "Issues and concerns considered outside the scope of this analysis".

Key issues, along with goals, formed the basis for developing and comparing the different management alternatives that were analyzed in the draft CCP/EA.

Some issues and concerns were outside the scope of this analysis. These were identified in the draft CCP/EA, but we will not further address them further in this final CCP.

Key Issues

Public and partner meetings and further team discussions produced the following key issues:

1. Protection of endangered and threatened species and other species and habitats of special concern.

This is the most important issue facing the Refuge Complex. Protecting federally listed endangered and threatened species is integral to the mission of the Refuge System, and is a common purpose for which each of the five refuges was established. Other federal trust species of primary concern include: migratory birds, anadromous fish, and certain marine mammals.

In the forefront of this issue is management for piping plover, a federally listed species (threatened). Piping plover nest on the beaches at Trustom Pond Refuge and Ninigret Refuge, and on the Narrow River estuary near Chafee Refuge. Block Island Refuge has potential nesting habitat; so far, nesting attempts there have been unsuccessful.

Threats from coastal development, disturbance by humans and pets, and predation are the major factors contributing to the species decline (Piping Plover Atlantic Coast Population, Revised Recovery Plan, 1996). Protecting piping plover presently requires an intensive effort by refuge staff who monitor plover nesting, manage public use and access on beaches, control predators at nest sites, and provide environmental education and interpretation about the natural history of piping plover and barrier beach protection.

Consistently each year, predators are one of the most significant factors affecting chick survival in Rhode Island. Also, since 1993, humans have caused three incidents of piping plover nest destruction: two were acts of vandalism directed at destroying nests and eggs; the third may have resulted from joy-riding on the beach. Campers often leave trash, which attracts predators to a nesting area, and often unleash their dogs, who chase adult plover off nests.

Some responses raised the continuing issue of restricting public beach use. Some feel we could do more to provide for piping plover by restoring habitat, or by working with the Rhode Island Coastal Resources Management Council (CRMC) to close beach intertidal areas.

Service staff help coordinate piping plover monitoring on nine beaches in southern Rhode Island, as well as on the refuges. This requires tremendous time and resources, both presently limited. Funding for plover work along the South Shore is inconsistent from year to year, and totally dependent on non-Service funding sources, typically foundation grants. However, the benefits derived are clearly evident in increased nesting attempts and productivity on many sites. The alternatives compared different strategies for protecting piping plover and managing important habitat areas on the South Shore.

Other federally listed species discussed are the seabeach amaranth (threatened), and sandplain gerardia (endangered), two plant species that may be considered for future reintroduction. The American burying beetle (endangered), which is known to breed on southern on Block Island, has yet to be found breeding on refuge land. Current levels of refuge management also emphasize other federal trust resources: Neotropical migratory birds, waterfowl, and colonial wading birds.

Appendix A lists species and habitats of special management concern. That list includes the status of all plants, wildlife, fish, and rare natural communities known to occur in Rhode Island that are federally listed as endangered or threatened, were candidates for listing, or are otherwise of management concern. Combined with location information, we used that list to identify additional land protection needs and opportunities. We know very little about many of these species' presence on or use of refuge habitats. The alternatives in the draft CCP/EA differed in their strategies for managing these species and habitats. Addressing this issue will help achieve Goal 1: Protect and enhance federal trust resources and other species and habitats of special concern.

2. Restoration and maintenance of coastal sandplain natural communities, including grasslands and shrublands (less than 60 years old).

While it is true that the Northeast landscape was primarily forested prior to rapid agricultural settlement in the 1800's, grasslands quickly became a dominant part of the landscape in the 19th century. Grassland-dependent species responded in kind and became established. Over the last several decades, however, coastal sandplain grasslands and shrublands, coastal maritime grasslands and shrublands, and agricultural fields and pastures, have been in rapid decline in New England due to a combination of development, changes in agricultural technology, succession to forest as farms were abandoned, and lack of a natural disturbance such as fire (Vickery 1997).

In Rhode Island, the State's farmland dropped nearly 50 percent between 1964 and 1997, from 103,801 to 55,256 acres. An additional 3,100 acres of farmland will be lost in the next 20 years if current sprawl patterns continue (Common Ground 2000). As a result, few large, contiguous grasslands and shrublands are left; only smaller, fragmented, and isolated habitat patches remain (<75 acres).

These smaller areas are unsuitable for many focus species, including once-common grassland birds such as grasshopper sparrow and upland sandpiper. Grasshopper sparrows have declined by 69 percent in the past 25 years, according to Breeding Bird Survey data (Vickery 1997). Our best available information suggests that grasslands should ideally be managed in 100 acre or larger patches. Smaller grassland habitat patches are much less productive for grassland birds, and could serve as "sinks", where species try to nest, but because of increased predation and other factors, productivity and survival is severely limited.

Other grassland and shrubland species have declined dramatically as well. Many of Rhode Island's State-listed plant and animal species are dependent on these habitat types.

Tremendous potential exists for refuge staff to become involved in restoring habitat on private lands. Grassland and shrubland restoration offers opportunities for our staff to provide technical expertise to local communities. The alternatives in the draft CCP/EA compared different levels of restoring and maintaining these habitats and providing technical assistance to private landowners. Addressing this issue will help achieve Goal 2: Maintain and/or restore natural ecological communities to promote healthy, functioning ecosystems.

3. Protection and restoration of the beach strand ecological community.

Beach strand habitat is in critically short supply due to its loss and degradation by development and shoreline de-stabilization. Meanwhile, the demand for recreational uses in these areas intensifies. The result is an alarmingly high rate of habitat loss and the decline of virtually all beach strand plant and animal species. Federally listed species such as the piping plover, roseate tern, northeastern beach tiger beetle, and seabeach amaranth depend on this habitat. The draft CCP/EA alternatives included different strategies for protecting it. Addressing this issue will help achieve Goal 2: Maintain and/or restore natural ecological communities to promote healthy, functioning ecosystems.

4. Control of invasive, non-native, or overabundant plant and wildlife species.

Each of the five refuges has an extensive distribution of invasive plant species. These plants are a threat because they displace native plant and animal species, degrade wetlands and other natural communities, and reduce natural diversity and wildlife habitat values. They outcompete native species by dominating light, water, and nutrient resources. Once established, getting rid of invasive plants is expensive and labor-intensive. Unfortunately, their characteristic abilities to establish easily, reproduce prolifically, and disperse readily, make eradication difficult. Many of these plants cause measurable economic impacts, particularly in agricultural fields. Preventing new invasions is extremely important for maintaining biodiversity and native plant populations. The control of existing, affected areas will require extensive partnerships with adjacent landowners, state, and local governments.

Thirteen invasive plant species affecting the natural communities within the Refuge Complex are considered of high management concern. The most prevalent are *Phragmites*, purple loosestrife, Asian bittersweet, autumn olive, and Japanese honeysuckle. Other species such as Japanese knotweed and multiflora rose are increasing on the Refuge Complex, and likely to become an issue soon.

Several wildlife species occur on the Refuge Complex that are known, or suspected to be, adversely affecting natural diversity. Issues surface when these species directly impact federal trust species or degrade natural communities. Mute swans are non-native, invasive species that aggressively drive native waterfowl and shorebirds away from nesting areas, compete with them for food, degrade water quality when they spend extended periods of time molting on coastal ponds, and are sometimes aggressive towards humans.

Native species such as deer, red fox, gull, and small predatory mammals such as mink, skunk, and weasel can be a problem when their populations exceed the range of natural fluctuation and the ability of the habitat to support them. Excessive numbers of deer are a threat to rare plant communities on the Refuge Complex, and excessive browse lines are evident on two refuges. Adjacent landowners are also concerned about deer impacts on landscaping, the increase in vehicle-deer collisions, and the threat of Lyme disease.

Red fox, gull, and some small mammals are voracious predators that can adversely impact other native wildlife populations. Occurrences have been documented of herring and black-backed gull, red fox, and weasel preying on piping plover and least tern, a State-listed species (threatened). Fox easily habituate to humans, and were being hand-fed at Sachuest Point Refuge. Many people fear fox and other mammals because they can carry rabies. These predators are particularly troublesome when their populations exceed natural levels. Control measures for each species are controversial, and may include lethal removal, visual and audio deterrents, or destroying eggs, nests, or den sites.

The draft CCP/EA alternatives compared different strategies for managing invasive species. Addressing this issue will help achieve Goal 1: Protect and enhance Federal trust resources and other species and habitats of special concern, and Goal 2: Maintain and/or restore natural ecological communities to promote healthy, functioning ecosystems.

5. Protection of biologically significant areas through acquisition and/or cooperative management.

Public meetings, partner meetings, and workbook responses expressed a great deal of support for the protection of additional fish and wildlife habitat in southern Rhode Island. That support runs across the State, as Rhode Islanders consistently vote ballot measures to maintain open space and protect fish and wildlife habitats. Many people mentioned that their support stems from their concern over the rapid pace of development on the South Shore. As we stated earlier, development in non-urban areas of Rhode Island has increased dramatically over the last 30 years. It is now the second most densely populated State in the country. One estimate predicts that current sprawl patterns will ensure the loss of all its rural areas before 2100 (Common Ground 2000). The Rhode Island Office of The Nature Conservancy has noted that the conservation actions taken during the next 5 to 10 years will be the most important for the majority of Rhode Island towns (The Nature Conservancy 2000).

This dramatic increase in development has changed land use patterns and practices, significantly modifying natural landscapes. As natural lands (those with sustainable native species populations and intact ecological processes) become isolated and fragmented into smaller pieces disconnected from other natural areas, their ability to support a full complement of native species is adversely affected. Cut off from larger populations, species and plant communities within these natural areas face the problems of limited genetic exchange, a decreased ability to support diverse populations, and lost capacity to recruit new individuals. Ultimately, the number of native species declines and exotic species gain a stronghold.

It is precisely this diminished ability of natural areas to support diverse species with different habitat requirements that leads to a decline in biodiversity. While some species can tolerate fragmentation as they prefer "edge habitat," many others, including "interior" dependent species, require larger, contiguous natural areas or functional corridors linking patches of natural habitat. This ability to protect and sustain larger natural areas and corridors, coupled with the protection of unique or rare species or communities, is critical to maintaining biodiversity.

A landscape or ecosystem approach to protecting land is also critical in the recovery of threatened and endangered species. Piping plover serve to illustrate this point. They have a fairly strong fidelity to certain nesting areas and typically return to them most years. Shifting of pairs between nesting areas has been observed when disturbances or habitat conditions affect their ability to nest. Barrier beaches are dynamic ecosystems, and their nesting conditions can change dramatically from year to year. While 1999 was a good nesting year on Moonstone Beach (Trustom Pond Refuge), in 2000, the beach consisted entirely of cobble with virtually no sand for nesting. The piping plover pairs there in 1999 appear to have shifted to the Ninigret Conservation Area. Without consideration of these shifts in habitat use across a landscape, management for these species would be ineffective.

Some individuals preferred that the Service acquire and manage federal trust resources, and that the Refuge Complex continue to acquire these sites. Others emphasized partnerships to cooperatively protect and manage important habitats not currently on refuge land. Still others recommended a combination of Service acquisition and cooperative management to provide the greatest long-term benefit to resources. At public meetings and in our workbooks, many responses suggested specific areas needing protection, particularly wetlands threatened by development. Some individuals we spoke with especially supported our acquiring land occupied by endangered or threatened species.

The alternatives in the Draft CCP/EA offered various levels of Service land acquisition, ranging from lands within the currently approved acquisition boundaries only, to a considerable expansion of each refuge's acquisition boundary. They also evaluated our increased involvement in cooperative land protection off-refuge. Addressing this issue will help achieve Goal 3: Establish a land protection program that fully supports accomplishment of species, habitat, and ecosystem goals.

6. Assurance of access to credible information about resources regarding the Refuge Complex to ensure management decisions are based on the best available science.

We need to determine and prioritize what information reasonably could be collected to facilitate decision-making using the best available science. In particular, many individuals expressed concern over the lack of information available to fully evaluate impacts to wildlife and habitats from excessive public use. Others questioned the effectiveness of management actions that have not been adequately monitored and evaluated. Several university researchers and other partners encouraged our staff to prioritize baseline inventory needs, establish monitoring protocols to better evaluate management actions, and identify information needed to determine each refuge's contribution to the ecosystem.

Implementing the Service's P*olicy on Maintaining the Biological Integrity, Diversity, and Environmental Health of the National Wildlife Refuge System* will require us to ascertain the natural conditions for each refuge and identify the natural communities, species, and ecological processes that are rare, declining, or unique. Opportunities to cooperate in collecting this information could be developed once the priorities have been identified. Addressing this issue will help achieve all the Goals identified for the Refuge Complex.

7. Management of public use and access.

The Refuge Improvement Act and Service policy require our enhanced consideration of opportunities for six priority wildlife-dependent uses (see above). Some level of each occurs on the Refuge Complex. Only those uses that are compatible with a refuge's purpose may be allowed. According to Service policy, all refuges are closed to any use until it is formally opened through the compatibility determination process.

The act also directs refuges to terminate immediately or phase out as expeditiously as practicable, existing uses determined to be not compatible. Non-wildlife-dependent uses exist on most of the refuges, and some have been occurring for years.

Public meetings input and workbook responses make it clear that public use on refuges is extremely important to most people. More than 90 percent ranked environmental education and interpretation and wildlife observation and photography very high as desirable public uses. Rarely, however, was there consensus on other public uses or just how much of each type to allow. Public opinion spans the entire spectrum from those wanting to open up refuges to non-wildlife-dependent activities, to those who want to close refuges to all public use to maintain an undisturbed sanctuary for wildlife.

The alternatives in the draft CCP/EA compared different levels and combinations of wildlife-dependent public use. Addressing this issue will help achieve Goal 4: Provide opportunities for high quality, compatible, wildlife-dependent public use with particular emphasis on environmental education and interpretation.

8. Hunting

Hunting surfaced late in the scoping process as a key issue, perhaps because, initially, few viewed it as a possibility on the Refuge Complex. This issue was raised by Service personnel, by RI DEM biologists, and by individuals both for and against expanding hunting opportunities on the Refuge Complex. Those in support primarily are interested in deer hunting on all refuges, waterfowl hunting on Chafee Refuge and Ninigret Refuge, and pheasant hunting on Block Island. Advocates of hunting refer to its inclusion as one of the six priority public uses that "...shall receive priority consideration in refuge planning and management" (1997 Refuge Improvement Act).

None of Block Island Refuge is open to hunting, but RI DEM has expressed its interest in any new opportunities for hunting because rapid residential development in Rhode Island is confining public hunting opportunities to fewer and fewer areas.

The Service views managed or administrative hunts in areas where there are overabundant deer populations as an effective tool for regulating them. The overabundance of deer is a concern in Rhode Island, reflected in increased numbers of vehicle-deer collisions, increased complaints about deer browsing on commercial and residential landscape plantings, visible impacts on native vegetation, and higher concern about contracting Lyme disease.

Those opposed to hunting cited concerns with public safety, disturbance and harm to other wildlife species, and the impact to visitors engaged in the other five priority public uses. The latter results from the likelihood that significant portions of the refuges, due to their small sizes and configurations, would be closed to other activities during hunting. Some expressed the opinion that the refuges should function as a sanctuary for all native species, and that hunting is incongruous with that function.

The alternatives in the draft CCP/EA offered varying levels of hunting opportunities, from no hunting at all, to opening four refuges during State-regulated seasons for deer, waterfowl, and pheasant. Addressing this issue will help achieve both Goal 2: Maintain and/or restore natural ecological communities to promote healthy, functioning ecosystems, and Goal 4: Provide opportunities for high quality, compatible, wildlife-dependent public use with particular emphasis on environmental education and interpretation.

9. Opportunities for environmental education.

Responses so frequently mentioned increasing environmental educational opportunities across the Refuge Complex that our planning team decided it warranted special recognition. More than 90 percent of the workbook responses ranked environmental education and interpretation as one of their top three interests. The alternatives in the draft CCP/EA compared different levels of environmental educational opportunities and the different levels of partnerships so integral to implementing them on each of the five refuges. Addressing this issue will help achieve Goal 4: Provide opportunities for high quality, compatible, wildlife-dependent public use with particular emphasis on environmental education and interpretation.

10. Provision of staffing, operations, and maintenance support sufficient to accomplish goals and objectives.

The Refuge Complex lacks adequate funding and personnel to provide the programs and services desired by the public and to effectively meet the goals for this CCP. The alternatives in the draft CCP/EA compared different funding and staffing levels based on their proposed management strategies for dealing with the issues. Addressing this issue will help achieve Goal 5: Provide Refuge Complex staffing, operations, and maintenance support to effectively accomplish refuge goals and objectives.

11. Increasing the visibility of the Fish and Wildlife Service.

Our lack of visibility on refuges was brought up repeatedly at public meetings and in the workbooks. Many people felt strongly about the need for more refuge staff to be present during peak visitation to increase resource protection and improve visitor services. Other recommendations to increase visibility included more visitor contact stations, increasing wildlife interpretation and environmental educational opportunities, a better location for a headquarters office, developing a Refuge Complex visitor center, improving existing visitor facilities (e.g., kiosks, interpretive signs on trails, etc.), increasing support for a volunteer program, and increasing community involvement.

Some people expressed an interest in seeing refuge staff enforce public use policy more consistently. Others argued it was unnecessary for Service personnel to be armed while patrolling beaches. The alternatives in the draft CCP/EA compared different levels of promoting our visibility and providing these services. Addressing this issue will help achieve both Goal 2: Maintain and/or restore natural ecological communities to promote healthy, functioning ecosystems, and Goal 4: Provide opportunities for high quality, compatible, wildlife-dependent public use with particular emphasis on environmental education and interpretation.

12. Need for improved facilities.

The Refuge Complex lacks a facilities plan establishing current and future needs for staff operations and visitor services. Many of its current facilities are inadequate. Its headquarters does not have enough office space to accommodate even current staff, and the visitor services area is limited to one rack of literature in the reception area. Alternatives in the draft CCP/EA compared opportunities for new or improved facilities to accommodate staff work space, increase the visibility of the Service and the Refuge Complex, and improve visitor services, including environmental education and interpretation. Addressing this issue will help achieve Goal 5: Provide Refuge Complex staffing, operations, and maintenance support to effectively accomplish refuge goals and objectives.

Chapter 3

Piping plover
USFWS photo

Refuge and Resource Descriptions

- Geographic/Ecosystem Setting
- Socioeconomic Setting
- Refuge Complex Administration
- Refuge Resources
- Cultural Resources
- Public Uses

Geographic/Ecosystem Setting

Landscape Formation

The movement of glaciers across New England created the land forms seen in Rhode Island today. The last of those great ice sheets occurred during the Wisconsin glacial period. Approximately 15,000 - 20,000 years ago, the glacier was in a state of equilibrium, where the melting rate of ice equaled the glacial rate of movement (Bell 1985). As the climate warmed 12,000 - 15,000 years ago, the glacier began its retreat, depositing pronounced land forms along its outermost edge. The southern coast of Rhode Island, including Block Island, is the farthest point the Wisconsin glacier reached in its southeastern frontal movement. The retreating glacier deposited rocks pushed by the front of its ice sheet in piles called moraines. These terminal or end moraines formed sinuous ridges up to 200 feet high. Block Island is part of the terminal moraine that includes Nantucket and parts of Long Island.

A second prominent moraine lies inland, the low ridge referred to as the Charlestown or Watch Hill moraine, stretching east to west parallel to U.S. Route 1. Glacial action also created other features in today's landscape: recessional moraines, outwash plains, kettle hole ponds, glacial lake deposits, deltas, and submerged gravel shoals. Prominent headlands like Sachuest Point are composed of glacial till, a mixture of silt-sized grains to boulder-sized deposits from the melting glacier.

Melting ice sheets caused the sea to rise rapidly across Block Island and Rhode Island Sounds until it reached its present level approximately 4,000 years ago. Wave action parallel to the shore continued to erode glacial deposits, creating the barrier spits. As the spits formed, they almost entirely sealed off the low-lying areas between the headlands and the ocean, forming coastal lagoons connected to the sea by narrow inlets. These became the coastal salt ponds we see today. Through the 1700's, all of the coastal salt ponds had direct, seasonally open connections to the ocean (RI CRMC 1984). The effects of erosion through time have shifted the salt ponds and barrier spits gradually landward (RI CRMC 1998).

The bedrock formations of southern Rhode Island include the Blackstone series of metamorphic rock along its southern coastal border (including most of Westerly, Charlestown and South Kingstown), granite rock of various ages (including most of Narragansett and Middletown and parts of Westerly and Charlestown), and Pennsylvanian sedimentary rock in most of south central Rhode Island (including Richmond, much of South Kingstown, and most of Hopkinton). Most of the soils around the refuges are fine sandy loams or silt loams.

Historical Influences on Landscape Vegetation

The upland forests of southern Rhode Island are classified by Kuchler (1964) as oak-hickory forest; while most of northern Rhode Island is classified as oak-pitch pine forest. Historic land use practices promoted this forest type.

As early as 12,000 years ago, Native Americans began occupying the area. Documented evidence places the first intensive occupation of the salt pond region during the late Archaic period (5,000 to 3,000 years ago). Native American camps from more than 4,000 years ago are known to have existed at one location along the shore of Ninigret Pond. However, societies of that time were primarily hunter-gatherer with little agriculture; broad changes to landscape vegetation probably did not occur.

During the Woodland Period (3,000 - 450 years ago), larger, semi-permanent or recurrently occupied camps became coastal settlements. Fortified villages are known to have existed in some locations. Maize horticulture became prominent, which likely resulted in small clearings. Larger clearings and burnings to control the movement of deer and upland birds may have occurred, and the first pronounced clearing of land along the coast for settlements, game management, and agriculture. Much of this land was cleared by cutting and burning, which favored resprouting by hardwood species like oak, hickory, and red maple.

The role fire may have played in shaping landscape vegetation is not well known. Evidence of fire has been observed in charcoal layers at Ninigret Refuge. Soil cores dug at most points on the refuge reveal charcoal below the historic farmers plow zone, approximately 10 inches soil depth. The dates attributed to these fires, coupled with their locations, suggest early Native Americans used fire extensively and purposefully.

Although small areas of land were cleared and more or less permanently settled by early Native Americans, it was European settlement and expansion in the 1600's that exponentially escalated the conversion of forests to agriculture. The eighteenth century Rhode Island plantation era "...required massive land clearing of the forests that had dominated the landscapes for the last 8,000 years" (USFWS 1999). During the mid-nineteenth century, an estimated 85 percent of southern New England was converted to field and pasture. Any woods remaining often were managed for firewood (Jorgensen 1977).

Block Island is similar in its prehistory to the mainland, except that occupation most likely began in the Middle Archaic period (7,000 to 5,000 BP). Human impact on the island's vegetation began with Native American settlement and accelerated during the 1600's, with "...European practices of land clearing for pasture and agriculture and the construction of fishing ports and associated villages" (USFWS 1999). Town records indicate the dominant species of trees on the island before extensive land clearing included white oak (*Quercus alba*), black oak (*Quercus velutina*), hickory (*Carya spp.*), and eastern red cedar (*Juniperus virginiana*). Beech (*Fagus grandifolia*), tupelo (*Nyssa sylvatica*), red maple (*Acer rubrum*) and sassafras (*Sassafras albidum*) were present, but less common (Hammond 1998). A detailed report on the archeological history of the Refuge Complex is available from the Refuge Complex office on request (Jacobson USFWS).

Contemporary Influences on the Landscape

The major natural disturbances affecting the coastline today are hurricanes and winter ice-storms. Hurricanes have the greatest impact, by far. The straight border of barrier beaches separated from the mainland by tidal wetlands and coastal salt ponds characterizes a coastline influenced by frequent storms. Wind and waves pick up loose sand and sediment and move it along the shoreline or back out to sea, allowing occasional overwash of barrier beaches and breaching of coastal ponds. Overwash, tidal currents, longshore currents, and rip currents are all mechanisms transporting sediment along the barrier beaches (RI CRMC 1998).

Fall and winter storms combining wind, rain, and waves are the predominant physical process shaping this landscape today. "Nor'easters" are well known along the New England coast in winter, winds generated offshore from the southeast, can actually be more destructive to the south shore, because of its exposure to the open ocean. The draft Salt Pond Region Special Area Management Plan describes the geologic, wave, and wind action for the South Shore, including details on how sediment movement constantly reshapes this dynamic landscape (RI CRMC 1998).

The Great New England Hurricane of 1938 was the most recent 100-year storm, one of immense power along the coast. Not only did winds reach speeds up to 240 miles per hour, but also a spring high tide created a storm surge between 10 and 15 feet. Storms of this magnitude are suspected to have occurred only four other times in recorded history: 1635, 1683, 1815, and 1821 (Bell 1985). Smaller hurricanes are less powerful but more frequent than the hurricane of 1938. Hurricanes in 1944, 1954, 1955, 1960, 1976, and Hurricane Bob in 1991 each left its mark on the coastline.

Human influences on sustaining the form and function of coastal landscapes and ecosystems over the long term are predominantly negative. Attempts to stabilize the beach system by constructing jetties or breach ways and planting beach grass have greatly affected the natural dynamics of this system by interrupting the natural flow of waves and sediment. In fact, the breach ways connecting the ponds to the ocean and one pond to another are the single greatest human impact on the ecology of coastal ponds (RI CRMC 1984).

Introducing non-native, invasive plants, diverting or draining coastal wetlands for development, converting uplands for residential use, and spilling oil are other significant human impacts on the coastal landscape. Recent studies indicate that the greatest threats to Rhode Island's estuaries and coastal salt ponds are septic systems and road runoff (RI DEM 1996). More studies are needed to establish the extent to which each of these factors influences Refuge Complex ecosystems.

On Rhode Island's upland landscape, a combination of management and natural succession has allowed forests to make a comeback. The State Division of Forest Environment estimates that 300,000 acres of privately owned forest plus 45,000 acres of State-managed forest make up 45 percent of the State's land area. Their estimate places 80 percent of the privately owned forest in tracts from 1 to 10 acres in size, which are difficult to manage as forest and are rapidly being converted to residential areas (RI DEM 1996).

Ecosystem Delineations

The Service emphasizes an ecosystem approach to conservation, typically using large river watersheds to define ecosystems. Rhode Island falls within our Connecticut River/Long Island Sound Ecosystem (Map 1-3).

Another commonly used delineation of ecosystems was developed by Bailey (USDA 1978, expanded 1995). These ecologically based map units often are used in landscape-level analyses. An ecoregion is first divided into a domain, then a division, a province, a section, and a subsection. Each level defines in greater detail its geomorphology, geology, soil, climate, potential vegetation, surface water, and current human use. Each of these resource attributes has implications for resource management. For example, opportunities to restore native grasslands may be limited by soil types, potential vegetation, and the extent of human impacts on the natural environment. Rhode Island falls within the Humid Temperate Domain, Hot Continental Division, Eastern Broadleaf Forest Province, and Lower New England Section.

Climate

Cold winters and warm summers with a moderating ocean influence characterize Rhode Island's climate. Winter temperatures average 30° F, with lowest temperatures ranging between -10° F and -20° F. Summer temperatures average 70° F, and peak in the 90s. Annual precipitation averages 44 to 48 inches, evenly distributed throughout the year. Thunderstorms occur throughout the summer (USFWS 1989).

Air Quality

The Clean Air Act establishes Class I, II, and III areas with limits on the amount of "criteria air pollutants" that can exist in pre-defined geographic areas. Examples of criteria air pollutants are smog (primarily ground-level ozone), particulate matter, and carbon monoxide. Class I areas allow very little additional deterioration of air quality (e.g. Wilderness Areas); Class II areas allow for more deterioration; and Class III areas allow even more. All of Rhode Island is currently classified as a Class II area. The U.S. Environmental Protection Agency (EPA) has designated the entire State a serious non-attainment area for ozone. That designation resulted in stricter automobile emissions standards designed to reduce emissions by 24 percent between 1990 and 1999.

Socio-economic Factors

The Refuge Complex lies close to some of the largest population centers on the east coast. The New York City metropolitan area, population 8.5 million, is 2.5 hours to the southeast. Metropolitan Boston, population 3.2 million, is 2 hours to the north. Hartford, with a population of 140,000, is 1.5 hours to the northwest, and Providence, population 161,000, is 45 minutes to the north (U.S. Census Bureau 1996 estimates; 1990 U.S. Census).

According to those estimates, the population of Rhode Island is about 1 million; 94 percent live in metropolitan areas (cf. the national average of 80 percent) and 6 percent in rural areas. South County, which includes Ninigret Refuge , Trustom Pond Refuge , and Chafee Refuge , has the fastest growing population and the highest number of building permits issued annually (RI CRMC 1998). South County population figures between 1990 and 1996 increased 7.4 percent, 4.6 percent, and 5.3 percent respectively in Charlestown, Narragansett, and South Kingstown, while Middletown's population decreased by 1.4 percent. The Town of New Shoreham, which includes Block Island, had a population increase of 10.8 percent. The population for the entire state of Rhode Island decreased by 1.3 percent over the same period (http://www.riedc.com).

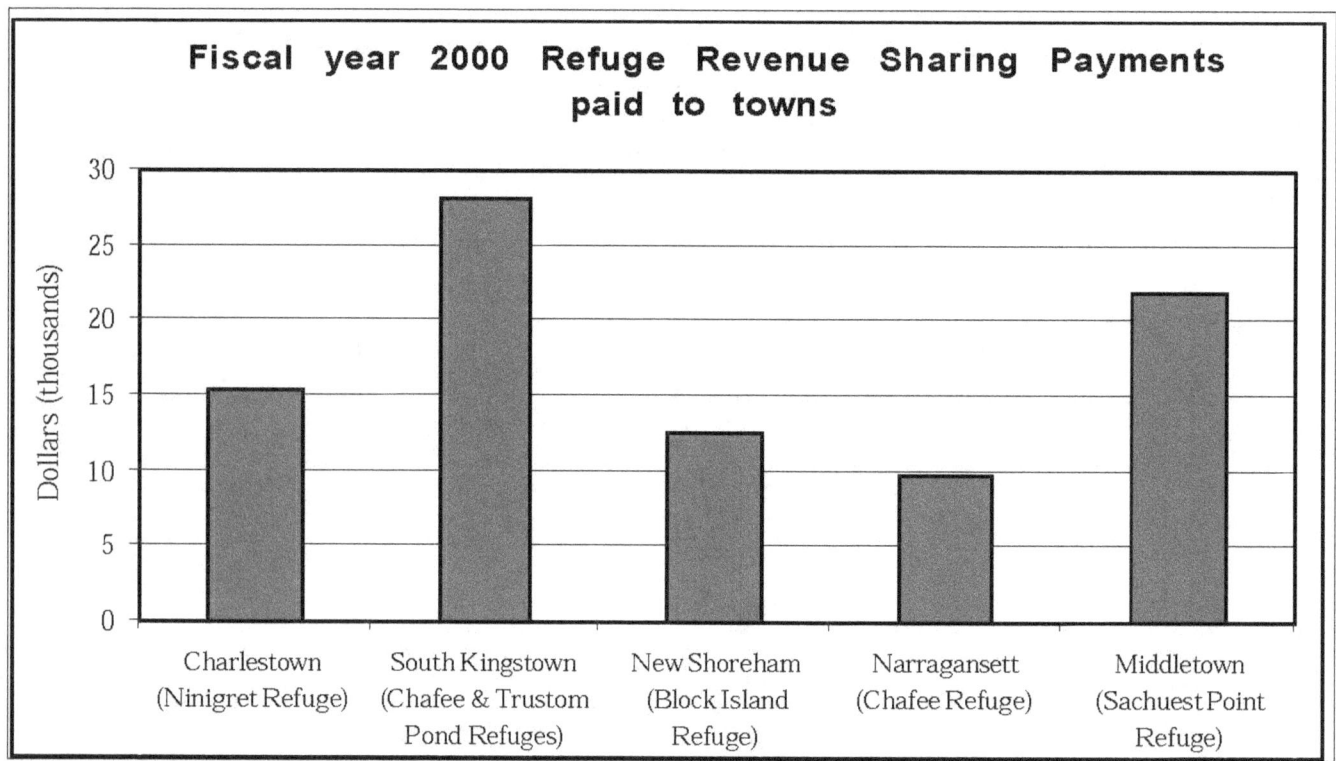

Figure 3-1. *Refuge Revenue Sharing Payments made to towns in 2000.*

The Refuge Complex directly contributes to the economies of Charlestown, South Kingstown, Narragansett, Middletown, and New Shoreham through refuge revenue sharing payments. The Federal Government does not pay property tax; it does pay refuge revenue sharing directly to cities and towns each year, based on the fair market value of refuge lands. The revenue sharing formula calculates three-quarters of 1 percent of the fair market value of refuge lands as the maximum amount payable each year. An appraisal updated every five years keeps their fair market value current. The actual amount of revenue sharing paid each year varies, depending on what portion of the maximum amount Congress appropriates that year (rarely the maximum). Figure 3-1 depicts refuge revenue sharing payments to those towns for the fiscal year 2000.

The University of Rhode Island Department of Resource Economics (Spring 1997) reports that travel and tourism is the State's fastest growing industry. In 1996, it generated $1.7 billion. The number of visitors to the State in 1997 increased at a rate twice the national average. Also in 1997, Rhode Island's services industry, which includes those in health, business, and education, comprised the largest wage and salary employment at 34 percent (RI EDC 1997). Between 1987 and 1997, the services industry increased by 37 percent, while the manufacturing industry decreased by 37 percent.

In all the communities surrounding the refuges, travel and tourism and the services that support them contribute substantially to local economies. According to Ann O'Neill, President of the South County Tourism Council (O'Neill 1999), the tourist season lasts from April through October, with peak activity during the summer months. Responses to our workbooks confirm that beaches and water-associated recreation are the primary attractions for visitors with destinations along the Rhode Island coast.

Current travel and tourism literature does not feature the Refuge Complex. According to Ms. O'Neill, its refuges are not well known as tourist destinations, although many visitors discover them during their visit and enjoy the scenery and open space they provide. They are small enough to explore in one day, and generally do not prompt an additional night's lodging. Ms. O'Neill stated that, since the Tourism Council is trying to showcase a greater mix of outdoor recreational opportunities in South County, the Refuge Complex will figure more prominently in future promotional material.

The greatest contribution by the Refuge Complex to the local economy comes from the values attributed to the preservation of open space (NPS 1992). We represent those values using three indicators, below: Cost of Community Services; Property Values; and Public Willingness to Pay.

Cost of Community Services compares the cost per dollar of revenue generated by residential or commercial development to that of revenue generated by an open space designation. On the one hand, residential development expands the tax base, but the costs of increased infrastructure and public services (schools, utilities, emergency services, etc.) often offset any increase in revenue. On the other hand, undeveloped land requires few town services and places little pressure on the local infrastructure. The cost per dollar of revenue generated by commercial land typically falls between those of residential and open space.

The American Farmland Trust (1989, 1992, and 1993) and the Commonwealth Research Group (1995) evaluated community revenues and expenses associated with open space vs. residential and commercial development. All available information on the New England States shows that open space and commercial development produced more revenues than costs, while the opposite was true for residential land.

Conversations with local realtors and appraisers helped us evaluate the refuges' influence on property values. Two South County realtors and one realtor/appraiser confirmed that properties adjacent to refuges generally are valued higher (Gross, et al. 1998). That value is realized through increased sales price/acre in properties adjacent to a refuge, compared to otherwise similar properties, and by how quickly those properties sell. Properties with views protected by their proximity to a refuge exhibit an even greater difference. All the realtors estimated, but none with any certainty, that properties adjacent to refuges may realize from 1- to 4-percent increases in property value. All the realtors we spoke with use a property's adjacency to a refuge as an important advertising asset.

Public Willingness to Pay is a method for estimating the monetary value of ecosystem goods and services by determining how much the public would be willing to pay, either in taxes, fees, or opportunity costs, to preserve ecosystem values. In Rhode Island, where coastal ecosystems are threatened by development-at-large, we have used Willingness to Pay to estimate the value of open space preservation.

Rhode Islanders consistently and overwhelmingly vote for bond measures to protect open space. Local and State-wide bond measures passed in 1985, 1986, 1987, and 1989, invested more than $100 million in acquiring land for recreation and open space. A State-wide bond in 1998 passed an additional $15 million specifically for protecting open space (RI CRMC 1998).

Refuge Complex Administration

Staffing and Budget

Table 3-1. *Refuge Complex staffing levels and budgets between 1995 - 1999.*

Fiscal year	Operations	Maintenance	Full time staff	Seasonal staff
1995	$216,299	$85,700	7	3
1996	355,715	23,900	7	3
1997	350,700	97,700	8	4
1998	428,400	171,000	8	4
1999	441,900	28,000	9	2

Annual budget appropriations are highly variable, and commensurately affect our staffing levels. Table 3-1 summarizes Refuge Complex budget and staffing levels from 1995 to 2000. Fluctuations reflect funding for special projects, moving costs for new employees, or large equipment purchases. Most of the funding is earmarked; very little discretionary funding is available.

Resource Protection and Visitor Safety

Law enforcement officers, with full authority to enforce federal regulations, are required to ensure resource protection and visitor safety. Three permanent refuge staff have been assigned collateral duties for law enforcement at any time during the course of refuge operations, but those collateral duties draw staff time and resources away from other important programs. We typically hire up to three seasonal staff with law enforcement authority each year.

During the past 5 years, formal notices of violation averaged 15 per year. They typically involved vehicle and pedestrian trespass, vandalism, and waterfowl hunting in closed areas. Well over 100 verbal warnings are also given each year, typically for inadvertently walking or driving in closed areas, littering, walking dogs in a closed area or off-leash, bicycling in closed areas, and digging plants. In 1993, a Trail Warden program began using volunteers to assist in documenting violations. Wardens also inform visitors of public use policy and permitted activities.

Refuge Complex Office

The Refuge Complex office lies in the Shoreline Plaza strip mall in Charlestown. In addition to housing our staff, it also houses our Division of Ecological Services Southern New England/New York Bight Coastal Ecosystem Program five-member staff, an Atlantic Coast Joint Venture staff person, and Friends of the National Wildlife Refuges of Rhode Island.

An environmental assessment was written in 2000, which determined a new location for a Refuge Headquarters and Visitor Center. The new building will be located on Deer Run Road (off Route 1) in Charlestown, RI. The building is currently being designed, with construction to begin in 2003.

Refuge Resources

Physical Resources

Topography, Soils and Hydrology

Glaciers deposited approximately 60 feet of New Shoreham drift, forming the island's hilly, morainal topography. Up to 3 feet of wind-deposited silt loess overlies glacial till deposits. Parts of Sandy Point were formed by finely sorted alluvial sands and wave and tidal shifting and deposition.

Terrain on the northern parcel, around the North Light lighthouse, is rolling dunes and swales averaging 5- to 10-percent slopes; soils are primarily sand. Beane Point is a 21-acre upland with <5-percent slopes composed of Paxton, very stony-fine sandy loams. The 13-acre Nevuus-Greenburg tract and O'Toole tract are primarily upland with <10-percent slopes also composed of Paxton, very stony-fine sandy loams.

Block Island's groundwater supply depends entirely on rainfall, with kettle ponds and wetlands perched on compacted, clay soils. The Nevuus-Greenberg tract contains two very small ponds; otherwise, no freshwater lakes or ponds lie on refuge property. Adjacent to refuge lands, however, are several small freshwater ponds, and the brackish Sachem Pond and saline Great Salt Pond. More than 365 ponds and emergent wetlands on the island provide a critical resource for many species.

Biological Resources

Block Island is unique from many perspectives, not least of which are its biological resources. In 1991, The Nature Conservancy selected Block Island as one of its 12 initial "Last Great Places" in the western hemisphere, primarily due to its ecological significance.

Our report, "Northeast Coastal Areas Study" (1991) noted the unique natural resources on Block Island:

"...one of the most important migratory bird habitats on the East Coast... [as it]...provides a critical link or stepping stone in the migration of many birds, particularly raptors and passerines, between southern New England and eastern Long Island, and points north and south."

The Nature Conservancy considers Block Island an internationally significant biodiversity reserve due to the presence of rare and endemic species and habitats, and because of the concentrations and diversity of songbirds, shorebirds, and raptors that migrate through the area. At least 15 rare, threatened, or endangered federal or state listed species, including birds, insects, mammals, and plants, reproduce on the island. Many additional rare birds pass through the island during migration.

Vegetation

Table 3-2 presents the dominant vegetation types and acreage for Block Island Refuge. Block Island Refuge is primarily upland, except for beach habitat at Cow Cove, Sandy Point, West Beach, and Beane Point.

Table 3-2. *Land use/land cover at Block Island National Wildlife Refuge, Washington County, RI. (source: RI GIS)*

Dominant cover-type	Acreage	Percentage
Agriculture	0.4	0.5%
Beaches	7.8	8.5
Brushland	20.8	22.8
Developed	5.6	6.1
Forest Upland	16.8	18.3
Sandy Areas (not beaches)	34.6	37.8
Water	2.2	2.4
Wetlands (not classified)	3.3	3.6
Total	**91.5**	**100**

Beach habitat includes bare sand, beach grass (*Ammophila brevigulata*), poison ivy (*Rhus radicans*), bayberry (*Myrica pennsylvanica*), wild rose (*Rosa rugosa*), and beach plum (*Prunus maritima*). Upland shrub habitat includes northern arrowwood (*Viburnum recognitum*), pokeweed (*Phytolacca americana*), Virginia creeper (*Parthenocissus quinquefolia*), and bayberry. A list of plant species is available upon request from the refuge office (George 1999).

Japanese black pine (*Pinus thunbergii*) has been planted extensively along eastern seashores since the 1940's because of its remarkable ability to withstand salt spray. But the future of the black pines on Block Island is uncertain. A mixture of bayberry and non-native Japanese black pine with a poison ivy understory dominates Beane Point. Those black pines provide important nesting habitat for a colony of wading birds, namely, black-crowned and yellow-crowned night-herons. Approximately 25 percent of the black pine on Beane Point has already been lost to an infestation of the black turpentine beetle (*Dendroctonus terebrans*). No attempts to treat the beetle have been made.

Native pitch pine (*Pinus rigida*) is also susceptible to black turpentine beetles and thus, is not a good replacement tree. Correspondence with Cornell University Cooperative Extension and Cape Cod Cooperative Extension suggest that chemical control of black turpentine beetle is not an option because of the proximity to water. At present, no native tree species resistant to the black turpentine beetle and tolerant of saline, shoreline environmental conditions is known.

Both the Nevuus-Greenberg and O'Toole tracts are characterized as shrub vegetation dominated by bayberry, arrowwood, winterberry, and chokecherry. The O'Toole property has a higher proportion of dry upland shrub.

Threatened and Endangered Species

Two federally listed species are known to breed on Block Island: the American burying beetle (endangered) and piping plover (threatened). The Service has completed recovery plans for both species.

Block Island harbors one of only a handful of American burying beetle populations, and the only natural population known east of the Mississippi River. This beetle is the largest of the North American carrion beetles, whose numbers have so drastically declined that they were federally-listed as endangered in 1989. As part of an attempt to establish more beetle populations in the east, the Service began a reintroduction effort in the early 1990's. They released captive-raised beetles on Penikese and Nantucket Islands in Massachusetts, historical habitat for the species. The western populations occur in a limited distribution in western Arkansas, eastern Oklahoma, western Kansas, central Nebraska, and southern South Dakota. Beetles have also been translocated from Arkansas to southeastern Ohio in an effort to re-establish the species there. Unfortunately, the American burying beetle remains absent from more than 90% of its historic range (Amaral 2000).

Surveys in recent years found the majority of the Block Island burying beetle breeding population in the grassland habitat on the southern end of the island. However, beetles have twice been documented on or adjacent to refuge land, including near Beane Point and just north of Great Salt Pond. In 1998, the town-owned fields just south of Sachem Pond were surveyed and American burying beetle were captured in low numbers. The beetles are highly mobile on the island, and in fact, could be found foraging in any of its fields today (Amaral 1999).

Beetles on the refuge are likely foraging primarily on dead pheasant chicks, and occasionally on dead gull and black-crowned night-heron chicks. Carrion availability may be the single greatest factor determining where the species can survive. Annual surveys and monitoring of the breeding population have concentrated on the southern portion of the island. Its northern portion, including the refuge, have not been surveyed as intensively.

In 1991, biologists placed the carcass of a herring gull chick on the Beane Point portion of the refuge, and later found an adult female burying beetle preparing the carcass (Amaral 1999). No other burying beetle observations on the refuge have been recorded. In general, the lack of suitable prey items, poor soils for burying prey items, and lack of grasslands underlie the inferior suitability of the north end (Kozol, et al. 1986). However, our New England Field Office recommends further evaluating areas of suitable soil on the north end before dismissing it as poor habitat (Amaral 1999).

Piping plovers attempting to nest near Sandy Point in 1996 laid eggs that never hatched. Field examination revealed the eggs had hardened, as if the birds had been off the nest for an extended period. In 1997, a pair of piping plover initiated nesting behavior, but never laid eggs. Piping plover briefly seen in the area in 1998 did not attempt nesting. None were seen in 1999. In 2000, a pair fledged two young on a town beach south of Beane Point. In 2001, a pair attempted nesting 3 times near the refuge. In 2002, a pair attempted to nest on Mason's Beach. No one has yet determined why plovers are unsuccessful here, although human disturbance and gull predation are possible contributing factors. The remoteness of potential source populations may also hinder reestablishment of breeding plovers in this nesting area.

Most of the suitable beach habitat for plover lies between Settlers Rock and the Sandy Point Tip. Other than a small stretch of refuge beach, most is owned by the Town of New Shoreham. Under a cooperative management strategy with the Town, areas of the beach between the North Light and Sandy Point will be symbolically fenced if piping plover are seen exhibiting courtship behavior. We will erect nest exclosures around any suspected nest sites. The staff of The Nature Conservancy-Block Island help monitor this beach during the breeding season.

Symbolic fencing consists of intervisible, 5'- to 6' high metal posts spaced approximately 100' apart. Each post holds a sign that reads "Bird Nesting Area." No physical barriers connect the posts. Nest exclosures are welded 2"x4" wire-mesh cages 10' in diameter that are placed over nests (typically just a scrape in the sand). Exclosures are topped with 1" black plastic mesh, and some sections have yellow nylon rope connecting their posts. The wire mesh allows plover to enter and exit, but excludes most predators.

A group of two to four immature bald eagles has been observed near ponds through the past five summers, feeding on waterfowl and fish; one roost site near Middle Pond's west shore has been documented. More monitoring is needed to document habitat use by these birds.

The 1994 Recovery Plan for the northeastern beach tiger beetle (threatened) identifies Block Island as a low potential reintroduction site (USFWS 1993). This species has not been documented in Rhode Island since the 1950's, but was known historically on Block Island's Crescent Beach. The nearest population of northeastern beach tiger beetles is near Westport, MA. According to Susanna vonOettingen of our New England Field Office, there are no plans to reintroduce the northeastern beach tiger beetle outside of Massachusetts for approximately 10 years. A source population to begin reintroduction has not been established. Also, the highest priority reintroduction site in Rhode Island would likely be the Weekapaug, Misquamicut, and Napatree Point areas, where the beaches generally are wider (vonOettingen 1998).

Some State-listed species also occur on the refuge. Thirty-seven black-crowned night-heron (*Nycticorax nycticorax*) (endangered RI) nests were documented in a colony on Beane Point in 1998, an increase from the 29 nests counted in 1996 and 1997. This population has been documented on Block Island since 1976; however, they did not move to the Beane Point location until 1985. Prior to this, the rookery was located on the south side of West Beach road and briefly on the south shore of Sachem Pond. In both of these settings, the rookery was in shrub habitat (Ferren and Myer 1998, Raithel pers com 2000). Nesting with the black-crowned night-herons are one pair of great egrets (*Casmerodius albus*) and one pair of snowy egrets (*Egretta thula*) (endangered RI). A few yellow-crowned night-herons (*Nycticorax violacea*) (endangered RI) nest nearby. This is the only heron colony known on the island. As stated earlier, these birds are nesting in a dying stand of Japanese black pine. Adjacent landowners have informed us that, before nesting in the black pine, the black-crowned night-herons used to nest in shadbush on the island. This has implications for evaluating how to replace the nesting structure provided by the black pine.

Three to five American oystercatchers (*Haematopus palliatus*) (endangered RI) also nest on Beane Point and occasionally have been found near Sandy Point. Sea beach knotweed (*Polygonum glaucum*) (endangered RI) is sometimes found near Sandy Point.

Block Island is the only place in Rhode Island where northern harriers (*Circus cyaneus*) (endangered RI) nest. A total of 15 nests occur on the island; up to six nests occur near refuge lands, but none have been documented on the refuge. Block Island is also one of only two places in the world where barn owls (*Tyto alba* – endangered, RI) nest in sea cliff cavities rather than in human-made structures or inland cliff crevices; however, none of the four known cliff sites are on refuge lands. No other nests are known for barn owls in Rhode Island.

Reptiles and Amphibians

Green frog (*Rana clamitans*), peepers (*Psuedacris crucifer*), and red-spotted newts (*Notophthalumus v. viridescens*) occur in the island's scattered freshwater ponds. Reptiles include common snapping turtle (*Chelydra s. serpentina*), spotted turtle (*Clemmys guttata*), eastern painted turtle (*Chrysemys p. picta*), northern water snake (*Nerodia sipedon*), eastern garter snake (*Thamnophis s. sirtalis*), northern brown snake (*Storeria d. dekayi*), and an occasional diamondback terrapin (*Malaclemys terrapin*). No surveys have been conducted on the refuge. There is speculation that some of these may be distinct subspecies, since they have been separated from mainland populations for at least 8,000 years.

Birds

With the exception of the gull colony and heron rookery, very little survey data exists on bird species and their abundance specific to Block Island Refuge.

The refuge gull colony, the largest in the State, has been surveyed since 1981 (Comings 2000). RI DEM, Refuge staff and The Nature Conservancy on Block Island have been monitoring the colony because of a concern the gulls could impact other native species through increased predation or physical displacement as they dominate nesting sites. Gulls are known to prey on piping plover chicks, and thus pose a threat to management for that species.

Figure 3-2 shows that overall gull populations have been gradually decreasing. Closing the landfill on West Beach and switching to a transfer station in 1990 probably contributed to this decline. Although it is important to note that gull populations are down

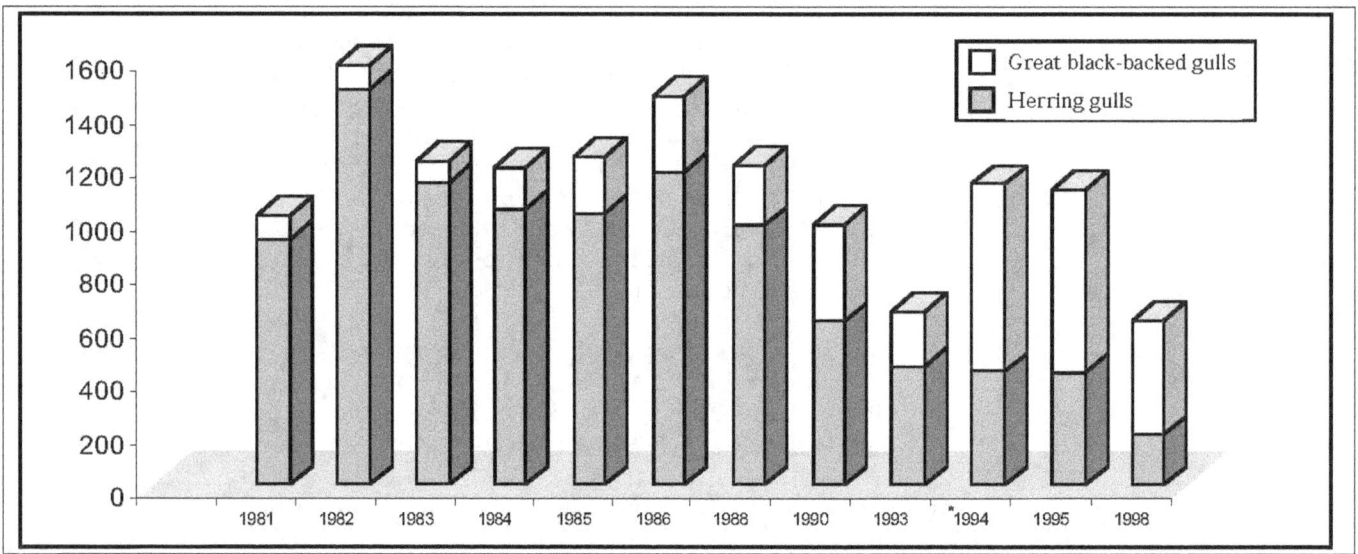

Figure 3-2. *Number of active gull nests at Block Island Refuge for select years between 1981 - 1998. (Data for 1993 represents only a partial count of the colony. No surveys were done for intervening years.)*

statewide, great black-backed gulls are systematically displacing herring gulls (Raithel 1999). In recent years, the black-backed gulls have forced herring gulls into the less hospitable shrub habitat for nesting. Unfortunately, black-backed gulls pose a greater threat to other native birds because they are a more aggressive predator than herring gulls.

While no formal surveys have been conducted for songbirds on refuge lands, The Nature Conservancy has two permanent banding stations on Clayhead Preserve on the northern end of the island. More than 6,000 birds representing 95 species are banded in a given year. This banding provides valuable information on the diversity of species breeding and migrating on the northern tip of the island. The habitat consists of shrub-scrub pine and kettle ponds.

Block Island is internationally famous among birders for its spectacular fall songbird migration. Data reveals that the island provides crucial habitat for both spring and fall migratory shorebirds and songbirds. Its northern tip, in particular, consistently supports large concentrations of fall migrants. Thousands of Neotropical migrants, representing 70 species, have been documented. Of interest is the fact that the vast majority of these fall migrants are juveniles. Studies indicate that juvenile birds are severely dehydrated by the time they reach Block Island, and that its approximately 365 small ponds and abundance of fruit-bearing shrubs provide life-saving rehydration. Many typically omnivorous migrants forage exclusively on berries while on Block Island (Parrish 1999). Northern arrowwood, northern bayberry, and pokeweed were the predominate fruit-bearing shrubs used by birds. Shrub habitat also provides resting shelter for migrating birds.

In his 3-year study of frugivory in landbirds on Block Island, Parrish noted that fruit-bearing shrubs important to migratory birds are superabundant on Block Island, evidenced by: (1) the fact birds never removed entire fruit crops; (2) interspecific and intraspecific aggression were uncommon; and (3) estimates of fruit removal ranged from 25 percent to 40 percent at individual sites.

Shorebirds pass through in large numbers during midsummer and early fall. Typically, 40 different shorebird species have been observed using the mudflats and saltmarshes and wrack lines on open beach, including piping plover and whimbrel (Comings 2000).

Mammals

Block Island is unique regarding mammals, because no native, terrestrial mammalian predators reportedly occur on the island. Feral cats and Norway rats are the biggest threat to small mammals, bird eggs, and chicks. No predator control measures have been implemented on the refuge.

Seals occasionally haul out on the refuge shoreline near Sandy Point; however, no formal surveys have been conducted. The Block Island meadow vole (*Microtus pennsylvanicus provectus*) is considered endemic to Block Island. Other small mammals include the white-footed mouse (*Peromyscus leucopus*), introduced muskrat (*Ondatra zibethicus*), house mouse (*Mus musculus*), and Norway rat (*Rattus norvegicus*). Since no surveys of bats have been conducted, we do not know what species, if any, use the refuge.

The overabundant population of white-tailed deer has been an important issue in recent years because deer are not native to the island, and there are no natural predators to control the population. The Town of New Shoreham and RI DEM administer a hunt program to substantially reduce the deer herd on portions of the island. Huntable acreage is limited on the island, due to limited access on private and public lands. Deer numbers on the refuge are not known, and hunting is not currently permitted on the refuge, but will be evaluated as described in chapter 4.

Cultural Resources

When English settlers first encountered Native Americans on Block Island in 1661, they described two large, permanent villages of 60 wigwams each and 100 acres of agricultural fields. Within the year, the settlers had surveyed and divided the island into lots. There are accounts of the settlers' enslavement of Native Americans to expedite clearing and construction. Native Americans disappeared from the census in 1875 (USFWS 1999).

No prehistoric sites have been recorded on Block Island Refuge, and we have not conducted any formal archaeological surveys. We consider the entire refuge highly sensitive for archeological deposits. The North Light lighthouse, formerly on the refuge but now on town property, is listed on the National Register of Historic Places. Archeologists have examined a 19th-20th century fishing village site on refuge property that has been impacted by coastal erosion and dune migration.

Public Use

We do not maintain a Service presence on Block Island, although refuge staff recognize the need for at least one seasonal employee to be stationed on the island during peak summer season. The opportunities for public contact are extensive, and include environmental education and interpretation.

Based on informal visitor counts (The Nature Conservancy 1998), we estimate annual public use on Block Island Refuge between Settlers Rock and Sandy Point Beaches at 40,000 total visitor days. No formal counts have been done. The Refuge Complex has not established a systematic strategy for collecting and documenting visitor use.

Principal wildlife-dependent public use on refuge lands includes surf fishing, wildlife observation, environmental education, and photography. We opened the refuge to surf fishing under State regulations through a Federal Register Notice in 1998 (50 CFR 32). That notice did not specify any geographic limits for surf fishing, and thus, the Beane Point tract was inadvertently included. With the exception of surf fishing, the Beane Point, O'Toole, and Nevuus-Greenberg tracts are not officially open to any other public use.

In 1994, refuge staff completed a compatibility determination for wildlife observation and interpretation, formally establishing these activities as compatible uses on the northern tract, near Sandy Point. That determination also found dog-walking a non-compatible use. Because of the lack of Service presence on the island, very little public use enforcement has occured in the past.

No public-use infrastructure is maintained by refuge staff. A short section of an unofficial, 5-mile hiking trail in the West Beach area crosses refuge lands. The North Light lighthouse, maintained by the town but surrounded by the refuge, is one of the most popular visitor destinations on northern Block Island. Access to the lighthouse crosses approximately 500 feet of refuge beach via a right-of-way. Vehicles use this right-of-way to access both the lighthouse and surf fishing sites.

Cooperative management of public use on the northern portion of Block Island strives to protect nesting piping plover. The Town of New Shoreham closed Sandy Point Beach from the lighthouse to the Point in 1996 and 1997, in conjunction with closures on the refuge beach after nesting piping plover had been observed. In 1998 and 1999, no nesting behavior was observed, and neither the town property nor the refuge beach was closed.

Chapter 4

Redstart
USFWS photo

Management Direction

- Refuge Complex Vision
- Refuge Complex Goals
- General Refuge Management

Refuge Complex Vision

We developed this vision statement to provide a guiding philosophy and sense of purpose for the five refuge CCPs. It qualitatively describes the desired future character of the Refuge Complex through 2015 and beyond. We wrote in the present tense to provide a more motivating, positive, and compelling statement of purpose. It has guided, and will continue to guide, program emphases and priorities for each refuge in Rhode Island.

"The Rhode Island National Wildlife Refuge Complex protects a unique collection of thriving coastal sandplain, coastal maritime, and beach strand communities, and represents some of the last undeveloped seacoast in southern New England. Leading the way in the protection and restoration of coastal wetlands, shrubland, and grassland habitats, the Refuge Complex contributes to the long-term conservation of migratory and resident native wildlife populations, and the recovery of endangered and threatened species. These refuges offer research opportunities and provide an outstanding showcase of habitat management for other landowners."

"The Refuge Complex is the premiere destination for visitors to coastal Rhode Island to engage in high quality, wildlife-dependent recreation. Hundreds of thousands of visitors are rewarded each year with inspiring vistas and exceptional opportunities to view wildlife in native habitats. Innovative environmental educational and interpretive programs motivate visitors to engage in better stewardship of coastal resources."

"Through partnerships and extensive outreach efforts, Refuge Complex staff are committed to accomplishing refuge goals and significantly contributing to the Mission of the National Wildlife Refuge System. This commitment will strengthen with the future, revitalizing the southern New England ecosystem for generations to come."

Refuge Complex Goals

Our planning team developed the following goals for the Refuge Complex after reviewing applicable laws and policies, regional plans, the Refuge Complex vision statement, the purpose of each refuge, and public comments. All the goals fully comply with Service policy and national and regional mandates.

Our Refuge Complex goals are intentionally broad, descriptive statements of purpose. They highlight specific elements of our vision statement and provide the foundation for our management emphasis. We identified Goal 1 as the top priority for the Refuge Complex; Goals 2-5 are not presented in any particular order.

Each goal is further refined by a series of objective statements. Objectives are incremental steps to be taken toward achieving a goal and define the management emphasis in measurable terms, where possible. Some of our objectives relate directly to habitat management, while others strive to meet population targets tied to species' recovery plans, or state or regional species plans. The strategies for each objective are specific actions, tools, techniques, considerations, or a combination of these, which may be used to achieve the objective. Objectives will be used directly in respective step-down plans, while strategies may be revised or modified to achieve the desired outcome.

Together, the goals and objectives are unifying elements of successful refuge management. They identify and focus management priorities, provide a context for resolving issues, and offer a critical link between refuge purpose(s), and the National Wildlife Refuge System Mission.

Integral to all the objectives under Goal 1 and Goal 2 is development in 2003 of a Habitat Management Plan (HMP) for the Refuge Complex. This will be the highest priority step-down plan to accomplish. We will write the plan using current resource information, but will update it based on new information, as needed. The purpose of the HMP will be to prevent the loss or degradation of habitat types, species assemblages, or natural processes significant to the Refuge Complex. It will identify habitat management actions that, to the extent practicable, restore and sustain viable populations of our focus species. The objectives and strategies identified below will all be incorporated into the HMP.

Once the HMP is developed, the Refuge Complex will develop a Species and Habitat Inventory and Monitoring Plan in 2004. Critical elements of the biological program to be inventoried or monitored will be identified, prioritized, and scheduled. This plan will also describe inventory and monitoring procedures, determine where data will be stored, and identify the interim and final reports to include. It will provide a critical connection between the HMP and credible, adaptive refuge management.

In addition, the Region is currently developing a Regional National Wildlife Refuge System Strategic Resources Plan (SRP). This plan will establish Regional goals and objectives for species and habitats based on landscape-scale analyses. Each refuge staff will then determine their respective refuge's contribution to implementing these objectives. As such, once the SRP is completed, the objectives and strategies outlined below may be modified.

The following goals, objectives, and strategies provide management direction for the refuge over the next 15 years. Unless otherwise noted, all work will be accomplished by the Service, primarily by Refuge Complex staff.

Goal 1: Protect and enhance federal trust resources and other species and habitats of special concern.

Objective 1.1
Sustain at least a 5-year average of 1.5 fledged chicks/pair per year (1996 Revised Piping Plover Recovery Plan) on at least one site on northern Block Island, with priority given to reestablishing successful nesting on the refuge.

Background:
The 1996 Revised Recovery Plan for the Atlantic Coast Population of Piping Plover describes the species status, habitat requirements, and limiting factors. The major factors contributing to the species' decline is the loss and degradation of habitat due to development and shoreline stabilization. The recovery objective is to remove the

species from the List of Endangered and Threatened Wildlife and Plants by: 1) achieving well-distributed increases in numbers and productivity of breeding pairs, and 2) providing for long-term protection of breeding and wintering plovers and their habitat.

Objective 1.1 directly supports Recovery Criteria #1 and #3, which relate to maintaining a wide distribution of breeding pairs, and a consistent productivity and fledging rate. In general, we hope to achieve this by increasing the amount and duration of protection and monitoring of nesting sites, and through habitat improvements, as outlined below.

In addition, the Partners in Flight Bird Conservation Plan for Southern New England (Physiographic Area 9; draft Oct 2000) (PIF Plan) lists several implementation strategies and management guidelines to achieve habitat objectives, including: monitoring and research, actively deterring predators, preventing human disturbance at nesting sites, and public education. All of these are incorporated as strategies or guidelines in Objectives 1.1 to 1.4 below.

No nesting has been documented on refuge lands within the last 5 years; however, nesting has been attempted on lands immediately adjacent to the refuge. While refuge lands will continue to be managed to promote nesting activity on the refuge, achievement of this objective necessitates a cooperative management strategy with adjacent landowners on the northern part of Block Island.

Strategies:

- Each year prior to the piping plover nesting season, continue to coordinate with and seek support from the Service's Ecological Services Division, RI DEM, and the U.S. Coast Guard.

- Each year, continue to monitor for piping plover in suitable habitat on refuge lands beginning in early April. Install symbolic fencing around potential territories (above the mean high water mark) to exclude public access when courtship behavior is observed. Place predator exclosure fencing around nest sites. Fencing will remain in place until birds have fledged (typically by August 15). Monitoring and management actions will meet or exceed the Service's 1994 Guidelines for Managing Recreational Activities in Piping Plover Breeding Habitat on the U.S. Atlantic Coast To Avoid Take Under Section 9 of the Endangered Species Act (Appendix G in the 1996 Recovery Plan).

- In 2003, annually close refuge beaches above the mean high water line to vehicles from April 1 to September 15 to reduce disturbance to nesting and migrating shorebirds and to reduce physical impacts to the barrier beach.

- By 2003, hire a biological technician, to be stationed locally, who will work with The Nature Conservancy to monitor suitable plover habitat, potential habitat, and public use activities in the Block Island Focus Area. This technician may also support other biological program activities.

- By 2003, refuge staff will monitor gull populations, in cooperation with ongoing RI DEM and The Nature Conservancy surveys, to ascertain whether gulls are limiting plover nesting.

- By 2003, formalize the current verbal agreement with Town of

New Shoreham, through use of a cooperative agreement, to insure continued implementation of town beach restrictions on public use when active piping plover nesting occurs. While developing this agreement, consider whether symbolic fencing could be placed on town lands on an experimental basis, in order to enhance potential nesting habitat on the adjacent refuge.

■ By 2004, hire a Rhode Island Piping Plover Coordinator* who will provide visibility and oversight to the Refuge Complex and South Shore piping plover programs, and facilitate interagency funding and cooperative management of off-Refuge nesting areas.

*The Rhode Island Piping Plover Coordinator will a) coordinate outreach and education; b) complete cooperative agreements with private landowners (see above); c) coordinate with towns to develop contingency plans (see below); d)coordinate piping plover research on the refuges; e) hire seasonal biological technicians; f) seek outside funding to help support the South Shore program; g) coordinate habitat evaluations and monitoring (e.g. determine nesting carrying capacities, habitat parameters to monitor, and predator trapping effectiveness).

Objective 1.2
Each year, minimize predation of piping plover at nesting sites in support of nest productivity and fledging objectives.

Background:
According to the 1996 Recovery Plan and experience at Rhode Island nesting sites, predation is a major factor limiting piping plover reproductive and fledging success. Predation is highly site-specific, but evidence indicates that human activities are exacerbating natural predation levels by influencing the types, numbers, and activity patterns of predators. As a result, we are managing human activities as described in Objectived 1.1 and 1.3, and also trying to influence predator behavior at nesting sites. Our predator management includes the use of non-lethal strategies (e.g. visual deterrents, scare tactics, fenced exclosures), as well as the removal of animals.

Strategies:

■ Continue to document statistics (productivity, fledging rates, nest losses, predation, etc.) in annual piping plover reports, and share information with Recovery Team Coordinator.

■ Continue to minimize direct predation of piping plover at each nesting site through the use of exclosures and other non-lethal deterrents, in combination with the removal of animals where it is warranted and feasible. Utilize recommended techniques in "Best Management Practices for Trapping Furbearers," a technical report to be completed by the Fur Resources Committee of the International Association of Fish and Wildlife Agencies, when available.

■ By 2005, evaluate predation statistics on managed piping plover nesting sites to determine the effectiveness of predator management efforts at each nesting site. Adapt management accordingly.

Objective 1.3
Within three years of CCP completion, develop a piping plover outreach and education program specifically targeting people using Rhode Island beaches.

Strategies:

■ Continue annual coordination with the Friends Group to provide oversight, conduct public outreach and education, and help secure non-Service funding for the Piping Plover Program.

■ Continue development of a barrier beach education kit for teachers.

■ In 2003, develop an education and outreach plan for the piping plover program, which will include:

  • Identification of target audiences (e.g. beach front landowners, elected officials, tourists, and local school children);

  • Distribution of literature with RI DEM beach use permits, and at beach access focal points;

  • A major exhibit at the new Visitor Center; and,

  • An educational program integrated with local school curriculums.

■ Work with the Friends Group and other partners to develop and implement the plan and secure funding for its initiatives.

■ By 2004, hire at least two additional seasonal Park Aides for the Refuge Complex to conduct outreach and education on refuge lands and in the communities directly affected by piping plover management.

Objective 1.4
Within three years of CCP completion, determine the site specific factors affecting Block Island piping plover nesting success and undertake actions recommended or accepted by the piping plover scientific community.

Strategies:

■ Each year, the Refuge Biologist will coordinate with the Piping Plover Recovery Team and other scientists to obtain new research results and share the effectiveness of management techniques.

■ By 2004, work with partners to identify piping plover research needs for the Refuge Complex, with highest priority given to determining those factors most influencing chick survival on the refuges.

■ By 2005, obtain funding to initiate the highest priority project.

Objective 1.5
Within five years of CCP completion, evaluate the suitability of refuge lands to support and sustain breeding American burying beetle.

Background:
The endangered American burying beetle breeds on southern Block Island, but has yet to be documented breeding on the northern end of the island. It has, however, been observed foraging on the refuge

and adjacent lands. To date, the northern end of the island has not been surveyed intensively for breeding habitat, and there is some question as to whether or not breeding habitat exists there. The Service's New England Field Office recommends further evaluations before dismissing the north end as poor habitat. High quality habitat would consist of abundant prey (e.g. pheasant, gull or heron chicks), suitable soils for burying prey, and grassland vegetation. Efforts to protect waterbirds (see below) will also benefit the American burying beetle through increased availability of carrion.

Strategies:

- By 2003, actively participate in ongoing annual monitoring of American burying beetles on southern Block Island, led by RI DEM, The Nature Conservancy, and our New England Field Office.

- By 2008, work with these partners to assess opportunities on the refuge to manage for burying beetle breeding habitat and expand the distribution of the island's population. If determined feasible and consistent with other biological objectives, initiate habitat projects on up to 50 acres.

- As lands are acquired by the Service, evaluate their potential suitability for breeding habitat.

Objective 1.6
Within five years of CCP completion, determine if specific management actions are warranted to sustain bald eagle roosting habitat on northern Block Island.

Background:
Over the past five summers, up to four immature bald eagles have been observed roosting on pond shorelines in northern Block Island, according to observations from The Nature Conservancy staff. They are attracted to the ponds to feed on waterfowl and fish. Of particular interest is the consistent observations on Middle Pond's west shore. More monitoring is needed to determine whether there is an established roost site that would benefit from additional management or protection.

Strategies:

- By 2003, a seasonal biological technician (recommended above for piping plover) will annually monitor roosting eagles observed on refuge lands on Middle Pond. Also, coordinate with The Nature Conservancy to identify other high use areas, and potential threats to roosting eagles, such as human disturbance and/or habitat degradation.

- By 2005, develop site management and monitoring plans, if such plans are warranted by consistent bald eagle use of refuge lands.

Objective 1.7
Within three years of CCP completion, determine if specific management actions are warranted to protect and sustain the wading bird rookery on the refuge.

Background:
Since approximately 1985, a heron and egret rookery has been established in a Japanese black pine stand on refuge land at Beane

Point. Between 1976 and 1985, these birds apparently nested in nearby shrub habitat, possibly shadbush. Up to 37 black-crowned night herons nests, one snowy egret nest, and a few yellow-crowned night herons nests were documented in 1998, All of these species are State-listed as endangered. Also nesting in the rookery are great egrets. This is the only known heron colony on the island. The Japanese black pine stand appears to be dying.

Black- and yellow-crowned night heron, great egret, and snowy egret are all species of conservation priority in the Partners in Flight Plan for Area 9 (PIF Area 9).

Strategies:

■ By 2003, utilize a seasonal biological technician (also recommended above) to participate in annual monitoring of the refuge rookery site on Beane Point. Monitoring is currently conducted by RI DEM and The Nature Conservancy.

■ In 2003, work with these partners to identify threats to the rookery and evaluate the condition of the pine stand supporting the nests. Determine what could be done to at least maintain the existing nesting capability. Evaluate whether to replant native vegetation. Identify and maintain prospective new sites so rookeries can reestablish or expand.

■ Use the North American Waterbird Conservation Plan (once completed) to update management and monitoring strategies for these heron and egret species

Objective 1.8
Within two years of CCP completion, establish specific habitat management objectives for those birds considered by PIF to be a high conservation priority in PIF Area 9, Southern New England, and for which the refuge could make an important contribution to their conservation.

Background:
Partners in Flight (PIF) Bird Conservation Plans are written for physiographic provinces with an overall goal to ensure the long term maintenance of healthy populations of landbirds. These plans identify species and habitats most in need of conservation, describe desired habitat conditions for these species, develop biological objectives, and recommend conservation actions. This plan covers objectives and recommendations for breeding, migration, and wintering habitats. Rhode Island Refuges lie within PIF Area 9, Southern New England. This PIF Plan is still in draft.

Although a final PIF plan is not completed, this CCP incorporates habitat objectives for certain landbird species identified as high conservation priority in the draft PIF Area 9 plan (Oct 2000). These include piping plover, shrub- and grassland-dependent coastal Neotropical migrants, and maritime marshland species. Using information from the surveys identified below, and the completed PIF plan, we will be able to refine our landbird management objectives in the near future.

Strategies:

■ In 2003, utilize the "Partners in Flight Landbird Conservation Plan for Southern New England (Area 9)" (draft Oct 2000), and the Regional Strategic Resources Plan (in preparation) to identify and prioritize those landbirds of highest management concern on the refuge, and assess how current management practices are impacting them. Determine which of these landbirds should be a focus for future management on the refuge, and write landbird objectives for the HMP.

■ In 2003, initiate an annual monitoring strategy for American oystercatcher nesting sites on Beane Point; identify potential threats and incorporate management recommendations into HMP.

■ In conjunction with HMP, update refuge cover type maps in a GIS database, adhering to the National Vegetation Classification Standards.

Objective 1.9
Protect and improve habitat quality for shorebirds at feeding and staging areas on the refuge.

Background:
Shorebirds annually migrate hundreds or thousands of miles between breeding and wintering grounds, often in one or a few long-distance non-stop flights. As such, migration staging areas, where birds rest and accumulate fat reserves before and during flight, are vitally important to many shorebird populations. Along the east coast, beaches are key locations. Long-term declines of shorebird numbers at migration staging areas along the Massachusetts coast have been attributed to conflicts between shorebirds and heavy human recreational use. Monitoring shorebirds during migration has not occurred on Block Island Refuge, so information is limited on whether it is a key staging area for shorebirds.

Strategies:

■ Use the U.S. Shorebird Conservation Plan (once completed) to update management and monitoring strategies based on any newly identified imperiled species (draft Shorebird Prioritization System 1999).

■ By 2005, determine if there are any key staging and feeding areas on the refuge, if so, map in a GIS database.

■ By 2006, determine potential threats and disturbances for key areas and implement a plan to reduce their impact. Use outreach and education and, if necessary, restrictions on public use and access.

Objective 1.10
Within five years of CCP completion, determine if specific management actions are warranted to insure seals are protected at refuge haul out areas.

Background:
There are no significant concentrations of seals known on the refuge. Generally, small groups of two to six seals will haul-out together. Both harbor and gray seals are observed on Block Island Refuge's Beane Point. Neither of these species are imperiled, but they are protected under the Marine Mammal Protection Act.

Strategies:

■ Beginning in 2005, work with partners to survey seal haul-out areas on the Refuge Complex and determine if human disturbance is a threat. Reduce human disturbance through public outreach efforts, and restrict access, if necessary.

Objective 1.11
Promote an appreciation of amphibian and reptile conservation, and actively manage to protect and sustain current populations on the refuge.

Background:
Recent studies conducted by the University of RI (URI) have revealed that Ninigret and Trustom Pond refuges are very important to the reptile and amphibian population in the South County area. In fact, the highest density of two amphibian species known for Rhode Island occur on these refuges. We suspect Block Island refuge could be making an important contribution to the reptile and amphibian populations on the island. We need more information on species' presence, and their seasonal use of the refuge, before recommending management actions.

Strategies:

■ In 2003, conduct annual anuran call count surveys according to Regional protocol.

■ By 2005, develop environmental education and interpretation programs to promote the significance of the refuges to Rhode Island's herptofauna.

■ By 2005, evaluate and incorporate recommendations (pending) made by Partners for Amphibian and Reptile Conservation (PARC) as warranted into refuge management.

■ By 2005, implement an inventory and monitoring plan for amphibians and reptiles of conservation concern predicted for the refuge.

Objective 1.12
Within 15 years of CCP completion, evaluate whether refuge lands can contribute to the recovery of the northeastern tiger beetle through reintroduction efforts initiated by the Service's Ecological Services Division, New England Field Office.

Background:
A Recovery Plan for the Northeastern Beach Tiger Beetle (*Cicindela dorsalis dorsalis*) was completed in September 1994. This species, which was described in the early 1900's as occurring in "great swarms", along beaches from Martha's Vineyard to New Jersey, is now only known in the northeast at two sites in Massachusetts. This beetle has been extirpated from the rest of Massachusetts, and all of Rhode Island, Connecticut, New York (Long Island) and New Jersey. This beetle is very vulnerable to disturbance while in its larval stage, which lasts two years. The larvae live in vertical burrows, generally in the beach intertidal zone, where they are sensitive to destruction by high levels of pedestrian traffic, vehicles, and other factors which alter the beach dynamic such as coastal development and beach stabilization structures.

Population growth seems to be hampered by a lack of both undisturbed beaches and of nearby populations to provide a source for colonizing new sites.

Several sites in Rhode Island were identified as historic and extant sites for this beetle in the recovery plan, and, while subject to change, their future restoration and reintroduction potential was also identified. Sites for Rhode Island include Napatree Point (low-medium potential), Block Island (low potential), Narragansett Pier (low to no potential), Roger Williams Park (low to no potential), and Newport (low to no potential).

Strategies:

■ By 2015, coordinate with the New England Field Office and RI DEM to determine the feasibility of reintroducing the beetles on the Rhode Island Refuge Complex or elsewhere along the South Shore of Rhode Island.

■ By 2016, develop site management and monitoring plans for prospective reintroduction sites on the Refuge Complex.

Goal 2: Maintain and/or restore natural ecological communities to promote healthy, functioning ecosystems

Objective 2.1
Within three years of CCP completion, design and implement a baseline inventory on refuge lands to determine the occurrence of species and habitats of management concern (Appendix A), and to serve as a basis for future management decisions.

Background:
To keep the HMP relevant, we will need to improve our general knowledge of important refuge resources, including their presence, distribution and condition, to insure management actions are sustaining biological integrity, biological diversity, and ecosystem health as required by Service policy (FWS Manual, Chapter 3, part 601).

Strategies:

■ In 2004, develop a priority list of baseline biological inventory needs to better understand and document the biodiversity on the refuge, especially the presence and distribution of species and habitat types listed in Appendix A. Incorporate these priorities into the HMP.

■ In 2004, begin inventories on the highest priority projects, incorporating the results into the CENSUS database, or other regional databases with GIS capabilities, to facilitate future analyses. Revise digital cover type maps as warranted.

Objective 2.2
Increase protection and restoration of 10 acres of beach strand habitat on the refuge, and promote the stewardship of these critical areas throughout coastal Rhode Island.

Background:
Beach strand (also known as barrier beach) is perhaps the most imperiled habitat type on or adjacent to the refuges because of the combined impacts of development and recreation. Many species

associated with this habitat type are either Federal- or State-listed as threatened or endangered. Protection, restoration, and enhancement of beach strand habitat and dependent species was identified as the number one priority in the Connecticut River/Long Island Sound Ecosystem Team Plan (July 1996). Management of these areas is extremely complex and controversial, especially when it includes restrictions on beach use. Block Island Refuge includes approximately 10 acres of beach strand habitat, with the potential for more to be acquired within the approved refuge acquisition boundary.

Strategies:

■ In 2003, close refuge beaches above the mean high water line to vehicles from April 1 to September 15 to ensure protection of nesting and migratory shorebirds, and to reduce physical impacts to beaches and dunes. The seasonal closure would not preclude emergency vehicles or use of the legal rights-of-way for the North Light Commission to access the North Light for maintenance and to provide access for visitors with impaired mobility.

■ By 2003, in combination with piping plover outreach and education, promote increased protection and stewardship of beach strand habitat through an intensive outreach and education campaign with the Friends of the Refuges and other partners to target beach front landowners, elected officials, and beach visitors.

■ By 2003, use two seasonal park aides to implement the project, who will be shared across the Refuge Complex.

■ In 2003, cooperate with the Town of New Shoreham, Block Island Land Trust, Block Island Conservancy, The Nature Conservancy, and Audubon Society of Rhode Island to develop a cooperative resource protection and public use and access plan for northern Block Island. The plan will identify strategies to protect sensitive areas (shorebird and waterbird nesting areas and native dune vegetation) while also providing for public use and access. It will also identify infrastructure desired to support compatible activities and evaluate a permit system and/or designated access and travel ways. Implementation will require a formal cooperative agreement among all partners. This plan will be incorporated into the Refuge Complex's Visitor Services Plan, to be completed in 2004.

Objective 2.3
Within five years of CCP completion, establish the extent of non-native, invasive plants on the refuge, the probability of new invasions, and treatment needs.

Background:
Issue 5 in Chapter 1 describes the implications of invasive plants becoming established on refuges. These plants are a threat because they displace native plant and animal species, degrade wetlands and other natural communities, and reduce natural diversity and wildlife habitat values. They outcompete native species and can readily dominate a site. Early detection and consistent efforts at eradication are critical to maintain control over affected areas, or to prevent new invasions. We are not currently aware of significant populations of invasive plants on Block Island Refuge; however, complete surveys have never been done. More information is needed before determining whether management actions are warranted.

Strategies:

- By 2004, treat invasive plants on the refuge pond just north of West Beach Rd. Also, identify and map the current distribution of non-native, invasive plant species elsewhere on the refuge.

- By 2005, establish an annual monitoring program if mapping reveals a major concern. Prioritize treatment sites to prevent new invasions or eradicate recently established plants. Highest priority will be to treat Federal or State-listed threatened, endangered, or rare plant sites or "pristine rare and exemplary vegetative communities" (March 1999 Invasive Plant Control Initiative, Strategic Plan for the Connecticut River Watershed/Long Island Sound). A maintenance worker will be hired to administer treatments; the position will be shared among all five Rhode Island refuges.

Objective 2.4
In 2002, complete a deer management plan for the Refuge Complex to address overabundant deer populations and evaluate recreational hunting opportunities.

Background:
Overabundant deer numbers are a concern on the refuge when they degrade habitat through excessive browsing or threaten human health and safety through increased vehicle collisions and incidences of Lyme disease. Since deer are highly mobile, it is difficult to effectively control a population unless they are managed throughout most or all of their range. The refuge has not closely monitored deer activities, including their impacts to refuge habitats. However, RI DEM has reported that complaints from citizens have increased in recent years about private property damage, worries of Lyme disease, and vehicle collisions. RI DEM recommends hunting as the most effective tool to manage deer populations on the refuge.

Strategy:

- In 2002, cooperate with RI DEM and the Town of New Shoreham to develop a deer management plan and environmental assessment for the Refuge Complex. The plan will evaluate hunting to help manage deer numbers and provide a priority public use opportunity. A separate public involvement process will be initiated.

Goal 3: Establish a land protection program that fully supports accomplishment of species, habitat, and ecosystem goals.

Objective 3.1
Actively strive towards permanent protection of all trust resources at risk on Block Island.

Background:
Consistently mentioned in the PIF Area 9 Plan, the NAWMP, Joint Venture Plans, relevant Species Recovery Plans, and Ecosystem Plans is the need to protect, restore, and enhance additional high quality coastal habitats to contribute to the conservation of federal trust species. While land acquisition by the Service and other state, federal, and local partners is a primary strategy for species conservation, each of these plans also recognizes the need to work in cooperation with private landowners to achieve conservation

objectives. Technical and resource support, outreach, and education will all compliment land acquisition efforts.

The Draft CCP/EA (Chapter 3: Developing Land Protection Strategies) described our method of identifying acquisition lands of high conservation priority in coastal Rhode Island. During the planning process we determined that the Service is the logical leader in coastal land and water quality protection along the South Shore and on Block Island, with the existing refuges serving as anchors. Refuge expansions will significantly increase protection of the ecological values on current refuge lands, while also expanding protection and restoration of significant coastal habitats. We completed a Land Protection Plan for the Refuge Complex (Appendix E) which identifies specific tracts for Service acquisition. The LPP incorporates the following acquisition priorities:

- Has documented occurrences of federally listed endangered or threatened species, or other priority federal trust resources;

- Lies contiguous to existing refuge land, which could further enhance or protect the integrity of refuges by assembling the land base necessary to accomplish refuge goals;

- Connects refuge land with other protected lands withing the South Shore and Block Island to help restore and promote the ecological integrity of the coastal wetland and beach strand complexes; and

- Protects and sustains important natural communities that can be managed tin cooperation with other conservation partners in a manner that will contribute toward refuge goals and the conservation of federal trust resources.

Strategies:

- Continue to assist conservation partners in identifying land protection needs, opportunities, and priorities on Block Island.

- Continue to help partners seek funding sources for their land protection programs.

- Beginning in 2002, expand the refuge acquisition boundary for Block Island Refuge by the acres approved in the Land Protection Plan (LPP; Appendix E). Initiate acquisition from willing sellers, in either fee purchase or conservation easement, as identified in the LPP, of 156 acres of high quality habitat.

Goal 4: Provide opportunities for high quality, compatible, wildlife-dependent public use with particular emphasis on environmental education and interpretation.

Integral to all of our public use objectives is development of a Visitor Services Plan in 2004 for the Refuge Complex. This plan will provide a coordinated strategy for implementing quality visitor services programs. We will emphasize the following six priority, wildlife-dependent uses identified in the 1997 Refuge Improvement Act where they are compatible with protecting wildlife resources: hunting, fishing, wildlife observation and photography, and environmental education and interpretation. The Visitors Services Plan will also accomplish the following:

- Establish strategic goals and priorities for Visitor Services across the Refuge Complex;

- Identify target audiences and partnership opportunities for each refuge;

- Establish a methodology for determining visitor numbers, capacity limits, limits on visitor impacts to wildlife and habitats, and a means for assessing quality of visitor experiences;

- Evaluate recreational fee opportunities; and

- Establish an implementation schedule for priority Visitor Service's projects.

We will hire four outdoor recreation planners to implement the Visitor Services Plan and staff the planned Refuge Complex Visitor Center (see Chapter 5- Staffing). As new lands are acquired, opportunities to provide compatible, priority public uses will be pursued, following guidance in the Pre-Acquisition Compatibility Determination (Appendix D).

The objectives below are designed to enhance existing, compatible refuge activities.

Objective 4.1
Each year, provide high quality surf fishing opportunities along the refuge shoreline, while minimizing impacts to natural resources.

Strategies:

- Continue to allow surf fishing year round on the refuge in accordance with State regulations. Some areas on the refuge may be closed to protect piping plover nesting sites, but generally, the refuge will remain open to surf fishing.

- In 2003, close refuge beaches above the mean high water line to vehicles from April 1 to September 15 to ensure protection of nesting and migratory shorebirds, and to reduce physical impacts to beaches and dunes. The seasonal closure would not preclude emergency vehicles or use of the legal rights-of-way for the North Light Commission to access the North Light for maintenance and to provide access for visitors with impaired mobility.

- In 2003, cooperate with the Town of New Shoreham, Block Island Land Trust, Block Island Conservancy, The Nature Conservancy, and Audubon Society of Rhode Island to develop a cooperative resource protection and public use and access plan for northern Block Island. The plan will identify strategies to protect sensitive areas (shorebird and waterbird nesting areas and native dune vegetation) while also providing for public use and access. It will also identify infrastructure desired to support compatible activities and evaluate a permit system and/or designated access and travel ways. Implementation will require a formal cooperative agreement among all partners. This plan will be incorporated into the Refuge Complex's Visitor Services Plan, to be completed in 2004.

■ By 2005, implement a monitoring plan on Beane Point in vicinity of the colonial wading bird and shorebird nesting site to evaluate disturbance by anglers during the nesting season (approximately May 1 to August 1). If necessary, public access will be adapted in response to monitoring results.

Objective 4.2
Increase opportunities for high quality interpretive experiences on the refuge, which raise visitors' awareness of the Refuge System and Block Island Refuge's particular contribution to protecting trust resources and significant habitats.

Strategies:

■ By 2005, develop an interpretive program for the refuge tiered to the Visitor Services Plan, and consistent with the cooperative public use and access plan. Evaluate interpretive opportunities in town center, on the ferry, or at the ferry landing.

Objective 4.3
Improve opportunities for high quality wildlife observation and photography on the refuge, while minimizing impacts to natural resources.

Strategies:

■ In 2002, formally allow access to the refuge for year round wildlife observation and photography. Restrict access to certain areas if piping plover are observed showing courtship behavior, as indicated in Objective 1.1.

■ In 2004, manage public activities consistent with the cooperative resource protection and public use and access plan developed with partners for northern Block Island.

■ By 2005, implement a monitoring plan on Beane Point in vicinity of the colonial wading bird and shorebird nesting site to evaluate disturbance by refuge visitors during the nesting season (approximately May 1 to August 1). If necessary, public access will be adapted in response to monitoring results.

■ Also by 2005, hire a seasonal Park Aid to provide guided walks; this position will be shared among other Rhode Island Refuges.

Objective 4.4
Increase opportunities for high quality environmental educational experiences on the refuge, while minimizing impacts to natural resources.

Strategies:

■ Continue to support The Nature Conservancy's environmental education programs on refuge land.

■ In 2003, initiate a formal partnership with The Nature Conservancy to facilitate sharing of resources and assist in curriculum development and implementation. A seasonal Park Aid will be hired for assistance (also recommended above). The Beane Point facility will be used as a classroom laboratory, and/ or housing for educators, researchers, or seasonal employees.

- All proposed environmental education group activities at Beane Point will avoid the sensitive nesting wading bird and shorebird areas, generally from May 1 - August 1.

Objective 4.5
Within one year of CCP completion, evaluate opportunities for deer hunting on the refuge.

Strategies:

- In 2002, complete a deer management plan and environmental assessment evaluating opportunities for deer hunting. A separate public involvement process will be initiated. (Also refer to objective 2.4)

Objective 4.6
Within three years of CCP completion, determine if incompatible, non-wildlife dependent public uses occur on the refuge and whether management actions are needed.

Background:
Incompatible, non-wildlife dependent activities detract from our ability to fulfill refuge purposes and often conflict with priority public uses and other management programs. Limited refuge resources should not be expended to manage activities that do not contribute to the public's understanding and appreciation of the refuge's wildlife or cultural resources, or to activities that do not directly benefit these resources.

- In 2003, increase visibility of the Service, and provide increased resource protection and management of public use, by establishing a consistent Service presence during peak summer visitation on the refuge.

- In 2004, implement a monitoring program to document public use (e.g. seasonality, numbers, types of activities) in an effort to determine whether incompatible activities are occurring on refuge lands and having an impact on natural resources. Utilize the seasonal staff recommended above in other objectives.

- By 2005, in conjunction with monitoring results and priorities established in the Visitor Services Plan, eliminate incompatible activities.

- By 2005, develop a cooperative agreement with the Town of New Shoreham to share law enforcement duties.

Goal 5: Provide refuge staffing, operations, and maintenance support to effectively accomplish refuge goals and objectives.

Staffing, operations, and maintenance needs are addressed in Chapter 5.

Map 4-1

Block Island National Wildlife Refuge

Public Use/Habitat Improvements

Comprehensive Conservation Plan

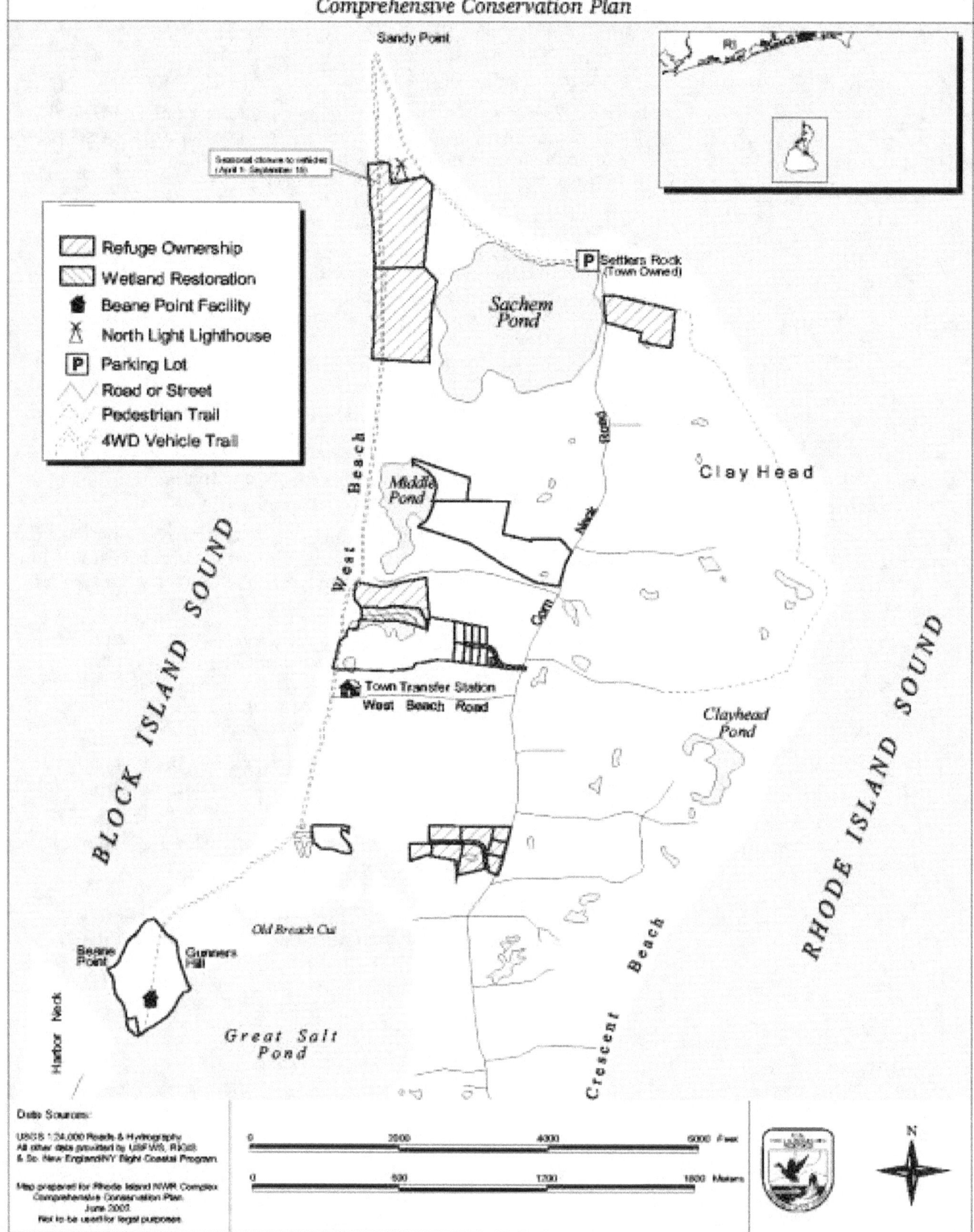

General Refuge Management Direction

The following management direction applies to all of the refuge goals and across all program areas. Some of this direction is required by Service policy or legal mandates.

Maintaining Biological Integrity, Diversity, and Environmental Health

The Service finalized its policy on Maintaining the Biological Integrity, Diversity, and Environmental Health of the National Wildlife Refuge System in January 2001 (FWS manual, Part 601, Chapter 3). This policy directs us, first and foremost, to maintain existing levels of biological integrity, diversity, and environmental health on refuges. Secondarily, we will restore lost or severely degraded elements of integrity, diversity, and environmental health on refuges where it is feasible and supports refuge purpose(s). To implement the policy on refuges, refuge managers are directed to determine: each refuge's relationship between refuge purpose(s) and biological integrity, diversity, and environmental health; what conditions constitute biological integrity, diversity, and environmental health; how to maintain existing levels of all three; and how, and when to appropriately restore lost elements of all three (Chapter 3, section 3.9)

The objectives and strategies laid out in this CCP generally improve the biological integrity, diversity, and environmental health of the refuge. Management actions emphasize maintaining current species and habitat diversity, recovering endangered and threatened species, and restoring natural ecosystem processes and functions. Implementation of the CCP will increase our understanding of the refuge's current resources, sustainable natural conditions, and the effects of our management actions. In addition, our strategy of adaptive management will provide continuous improvement toward meeting this policy's intent.

Protecting and Managing Cultural Resources

By law, we must consider the effects of our actions on archeological and historic resources. We will comply with Section 106 of the National Historic Preservation Act before disturbing any ground. Compliance may require any or all of the following: a State Historic Preservation Records survey, literature survey, or field survey.

In addition to basic compliance requirements, we will undertake the following projects to better protect and interpret cultural resources on the refuge:

- By 2005, initiate a cultural resources overview of the Refuge Complex to increase the available data on cultural resources.

- Also by 2005, develop a Memorandum of Understanding (MOU) with the Narragansett Indian Tribal Council to facilitate cooperation on environmental education and interpretation, to improve our understanding of the context of natural resources, and to increase site identification and protection.

- By 2006, train at least one law enforcement officer on the refuge in regulations associated with the Archeological Resources Protection Act (ARPA).

Tribal Coordination

Increasing communication with the Narragansett Indian Tribal Council is very important for the Refuge Complex. As noted above, we plan to develop an MOU by 2005 to establish a mutually beneficial working relationship that includes cooperating in environmental education and interpretation and protecting cultural resources.

Coastal Resources Management Council Coordination

The federal Coastal Zone Management Act (16 U.S.C. §1451, as amended) requires the Service to work with the State Coastal Resources Management Council (CRMC) to insure refuge programs and activities are consistent to the maximum extent practicable with the enforceable policies adopted by the state. The CRMC's concurrence with the Service's Federal Consistency Determination on the CCP was predicated on meeting the following management direction:

1) Provide Separate Consistency Determinations for Major Construction Projects. Major construction projects such as buildings, parking lots, roads, and boardwalks, which the Service determines may effect coastal resources, will require separate federal consistency determinations for each project.

2) Annual Coordination Meetings. Refuge Complex and CRMC staff will meet at least once annually to review general plans and projects which the Service has determined may effect coastal resources. These meetings will cover proposals for the forthcoming calendar year. The objective of these meetings will be to provide CRMC staff with available details on what is being proposed and to address their concerns. It is mutually understood that some projects may not be fully developed at the time of meeting.

Refuge Revenue Sharing Payments

Annual refuge revenue sharing payments to the Town of New Shoreham will continue. Future increases in payments will be commensurate with increases in the appraised fair market values of refuge lands, new acquisitions of land, and new Congressional appropriations.

Controlling Mosquitos

Within the past few years, incidences of mosquito-borne Eastern Equine Encephalitis and West Nile virus have elevated public health concerns about mosquito control in the Middle Atlantic States. Mosquito control has been very limited on the Refuge Complex, and has occurred only on the mainland refuges at the direct request of the State's Mosquito Abatement Office. During the last 5 years, we used two very localized applications of the larvicide Bti on two problem breeding sites. Our Regional Contaminants Specialist pre-approved those applications.

In general, we will not use larvicides on the Refuge Complex to control mosquitos. However, in cooperation with neighboring towns and the Mosquito Abatement Office, we will consider applying larvicides on a case-by-case basis, particularly when there is an elevated public health risk. The Service is now evaluating this issue on a regional basis, and has begun preparation for an environmental impact statement. This may result in Service policy or Regional guidelines being developed and incorporated into this CCP in the future.

Permitting Special Use (including Research)

Requests for special use permits will be evaluated by the Refuge Manager on a case-by-case. All permitted activities must be determined appropriate and compatible through a compatibility determination. At a minimum, all commercial activities and all research projects require a special use permit. Research projects that will improve and strengthen natural resource management decisions on the Refuge Complex will generally be approved. The Refuge Manager will encourage partnerships with local universities and colleges to facilitate research that will help evaluate CCP objectives and strategies, or the assumptions on which they are based.

The Refuge Manager may also consider research not directly related to refuge objectives, but which contributes to the broader enhancement, protection, or management of native species and biological diversity within the region.

Each refuge will maintain a list of research needs to provide prospective researchers or organizations upon request. The Refuge Manager will determine on a case-by-case basis whether they can directly support a project through funding, in-kind services (e.g. housing or use of other facilities), field assistance, or through sharing data and records. Research results will be shared within the Service, and with RI DEM.

All researchers on refuges, current and future, are required to submit a detailed research proposal following Service policy in the FWS Refuge Manual, Chapter 4 Section 6. Special use permits must also identify a schedule for progress reports (at least annual), criteria for determining when a project should cease, and publication or other final reporting requirements. The Regional Refuge Biologists, other Service divisions, and state agencies will be asked to review and comment on research proposals.

Some projects, such as depredation and banding studies, require additional Service permits. These projects will not be approved until all Service permits and Endangered Species Act consultation requirements are met. Also, to maintain the natural landscape of the refuge, projects which require permanent or semi-permanent structures will not be allowed, except for extenuating circumstances unforseen at this time.

Chapter 5

Laughing gull
USFWS photo

Implementation and Monitoring

- Refuge Complex Staffing
- Refuge Complex Funding
- Step-down Management Plans
- Partnerships
- Volunteer Program
- Maintaining Existing Facilities
- Monitoring and Evaluation
- Adaptive Management
- Compatibility Determinations
- Additional NEPA Analysis
- Plan Amendment and Revision

Refuge Complex Staffing

The five Rhode Island Refuges are managed as a Refuge Complex, with centrally stationed staff taking on duties at multiple refuges. A total of 26 full time personnel, one Student-to-Career Experience Program (SCEP) trainee, and 17 seasonal personnel, are needed to fully implement all five Refuge CCPs. Permanent staff serving all five refuges may be stationed at the Refuge Headquarters in Charlestown, RI, or at Sachuest Point Refuge in Middletown, RI. Some permanent and temporary staff may be stationed seasonally on Block Island Refuge. Appendix G identifies currently filled positions, recommended new positions, and the overall supervisory structure. The new positions identified will increase visitor services, biological expertise, and visibility of the Service on refuge lands.

Refuge Complex Funding

Successful implementation of the CCPs for each refuge relies on our ability to secure funding, personnel, infrastructure, and other resources to accomplish the actions identified. Full implementation of the actions and strategies in all five Refuge Complex CCPs would incur one-time costs of $8.9 million. This includes staffing, major construction projects, and individual resource program expansions. Most of these projects have been identified as Tier 1 or Tier 2 Projects in the National Wildlife Refuge System's Refuge Operations Needs System database (RONS). Appendix F lists RONS projects and their recurring costs, such as salaries, following the first year. Also presented in Appendix F is a list of projects in the Service's current Maintenance Management System (MMS) database for the Refuge Complex. Currently, the MMS database lists $3.85 million in maintaenance needs for the Refuge Complex.

Land acquisition costs are identified separately. The Land Protection Plan (LPP, Appendix E) expanded the Refuge Complex acquisition boundary by 2,681, increasing the total unacquired acreage to 3,130. We estimate the value of these lands to be $83 million at current, fair-market prices. In all probability, the Refuge Complex will protect these lands at a lower cost, as some parcels may be protected through conservation easements or acquired through donation or land exchange.

Step-Down Management Plans

The Refuge System Manual (Part 4 Chapter 3) lists more than 25 Step-Down Management Plans generally required on most refuges. Step-down plans describe specific management actions a refuge will follow to achieve objectives or implement management strategies. Some require annual revision, others are revised on a 5- to 10-year schedule. Some require additional NEPA analysis, public involvement, and compatibility determinations before they can be implemented. A status list of Rhode Island Refuge Complex step-down plans follows.

These plans are current :

- Fire Management Plan, 1995 (Refuge Complex); updated with annual burn plans

- Grasslands Management Plan, 1994 (Trustom Pond Refuge); will be incorporated into the Habitat Management Plan for the Refuge Complex in 2003

- Continuity of Operations Plan, 1998 (Refuge Complex)

- Animal Control Plan, 1995 (Refuge Complex); will be updated with Integrated Predator Management and Trapping Plans for the Refuge Complex

These plans are now in draft form or being prepared:

- Safety Program and Operations Plan (Refuge Complex)

- Law Enforcement Plan (Refuge Complex)

These plans exist, but we consider them out-of-date and needing revisions as indicated:

- Water Management Plan (Trustom Pond Refuge); incorporate into Habitat Management Plan by 2003

- Hunting Plan (Trustom Pond Refuge); incorporate into Hunt Plan for the Refuge Complex in 2003

- Sign Plan (Refuge Complex); expand to Facilities and Sign Plan by 2005

- Croplands Management Plan (Trustom Pond Refuge); incorporate into Habitat Management Plan for Refuge Complex in 2003

These step-down plans need to be initiated and will be completed by the indicated dates:

- Refuge Complex Habitat Management Plan (highest priority step down plan) in 2003

- Refuge Complex Hunt Plan in 2003

- Refuge Complex Species and Habitat Inventory and Monitoring Plan in 2004

- Integrated Predator Management Plan in 2004

- Refuge Complex Visitor Services Plan in 2004

- Fishing Plan by 2005

- Trapping Plan by 2004

Partnerships

The Refuge Complex staff is proud of its long history of partnerships. More than 45 partnerships have supported the refuges, including four universities and colleges, numerous departments within Rhode Island State government, town administrations, conservation commissions, school districts, conservation groups and land trusts, environmental education centers, historic preservation groups, adjacent landowners, and other federal agencies. These partnerships have resulted in biological research, cooperative management of threatened and endangered species and declining habitats, protection of open space, and environmental education programs.

Refuge staff were particularly delighted by the establishment in 1998 of a "Friends of the National Wildlife Refuges of Rhode Island" group. The Friends are a non-profit advocacy group dedicated to supporting Refuge Complex goals within the community through public education and interpretation, project funding, and volunteer coordination. Their mission is "…[to be] devoted to the conservation and development of needed healthy habitat for flora and fauna at the National Wildlife Refuges of Rhode Island and to the provision of a safe, accessible ecological experience for our visitors…."

We will strengthen and formalize refuge partnerships to promote coordinated management and facilitate sharing of resources. Our partnership with the Friends Group is vitally important to us for community relations and for support in implementing our resource programs. Partnerships help us build support for the refuge, facilitate the sharing of information, and supplement the efforts of refuge staff.

Strategies:

- By 2003, we will conduct at least semi-annual meetings with the Friends Group to promote communication and evaluate implementation of the MOU. We will continue to actively support and promote the Friends Group's vital efforts in funding and implementing outreach and environmental education programs, which enhance our ability to meet refuge goals.

- By 2005, develop formal agreements with current partners, such as the Town of New Shoreham, Block Island Land Trust, Block Island Conservancy, The Nature Conservancy on Block Island, to identify mutual goals, and opportunities for cost sharing, technical exchange, and environmental education and interpretation.

Volunteer Program

Volunteers are vital to accomplishing all Refuge Complex goals. For example, in fiscal years 2000 and 2001, volunteers donated 9,332 and 10,000 hours respectively, assisting in environmental education programs, monitoring public use, maintaining facilities, and managing habitats. This translates to more than $110,000 worth of services contributed to the refuges in 2000 and $117,900 in 2001. Volunteers are also largely responsible for staffing the visitor contact station at Trustom Pond Refuge.

In 1999 we hired a permanent staff Volunteer Coordinator to improve the quality of the program through better coordination, supervision and training of volunteers, and to better integrate volunteers into all refuge programs. The coordinator compiles and distributes a quarterly newsletter to volunteers, refuge partners, and interest groups, keeping them informed about management activities and upcoming interpretive programs on the Refuge Complex.

Maintaining Existing Facilities

Periodic maintenance of existing facilities is critical to ensure safety and accessibility for Refuge Complex staff and visitors. Existing facilities include the Trustom Pond Refuge visitor contact station, Refuge Complex maintenance compound, and numerous parking areas, observation platforms, and trails. Many of these facilities are not currently Americans With Disabilities Act (ADA) compliant; upgrading is needed. Appendix F displays the fiscal year (FY) 2000 Maintenance Management System (MMS) database list of backlogged maintenance entries for the Refuge Complex.

We will also undertake the following strategies to improve the visibility of the Service:

- By 2005, complete construction of the Visitor Center/Headquarters for the Refuge Complex, implementing recommendations for interior facility design from the August 1999 Project Identification Document. At least one Visitor Services Specialist will be hired to administer the new facility.
- By 2005, complete a Refuge Complex Facilities and Sign Plan.

Monitoring and Evaluation

Monitoring and Evaluation for this CCP will occur at two levels. The first level, which we refer to as implementation monitoring, responds to the question, "Did we do what we said we would do, when we said we would do it?" Annual implementation monitoring will be achieved by using the checklist in Appendix H for the Refuge Complex.

The second level of monitoring, which we refer to as effectiveness monitoring, responds to the question, "Are the actions we proposed effective in achieving the results we had hoped for?" Or, in other words, "Are the actions leading us toward our vision, goals, and objectives?" Effectiveness monitoring evaluates an individual action, a suite of actions, or an entire resource program. This approach is more analytical in evaluating management effects on species, populations, habitats, refuge visitors, ecosystem integrity, or the socio-economic environment. More often, the criteria to monitor and evaluate these management effects will be established in step-down, individual project, or cooperator plans, or through the research program. The Species and Habitat Inventory and Monitoring Plan, to be completed in 2004, will be based on the needs and priorities identified in the Habitat Management Plan.

Adaptive Management

This CCP is a dynamic document. A strategy of adaptive management will keep it relevant and current. Through scientific research, inventories and monitoring, and our management experiences, we will gain new information which may alter our course of action. We acknowledge that our information on species, habitats, and ecosystems is incomplete, provisional, and subject to change as our knowledge base improves.
Objectives and strategies must be adaptable in responding to new information and spatial and temporal changes. We will continually evaluate management actions, through monitoring or research, to

reconsider whether their original assumptions and predictions are still valid. In this way, management becomes an active process of learning "what really works". It is important that the public understand and appreciate the adaptive nature of natural resource management.

The Refuge Manager is responsible for changing management actions or objectives if they do not produce the desired conditions. Significant changes may warrant additional NEPA analysis; minor changes will not, but will be documented in annual monitoring, project evaluation reports, or the annual refuge narratives.

Compatibility Determinations

Federal law and policy provide the direction and planning framework to protect the Refuge System from incompatible or harmful human activities and to insure that Americans can enjoy Refuge System lands and waters. The National Wildlife Refuge System Administration Act of 1966, as amended by the National Wildlife Refuge System Improvement Act of 1997, is the key legislation on managing public uses and compatibility.

Before activities or uses are allowed on a National Wildlife Refuge, we must determine that each is a "compatible use." A compatible use is a use that, based on the sound professional judgement of the Refuge Manager, " ...will not materially interfere with or detract from the fulfillment of the mission of the Refuge System or the purposes of the refuge." "Wildlife-dependent recreational uses may be authorized on a refuge when they are compatible and not inconsistent with public safety. Except for consideration of consistency with State laws and regulations as provided for in section (m), no other determinations or findings are required to be made by the refuge official under this Act or the Refuge Recreation Act for wildlife-dependent recreation to occur." (Refuge Improvement Act)

Compatibility determinations were distributed (in the draft CCP/EA) for a 51 day public review in early 2001. These determinations have since been approved, and will allow the continuation of the following public use programs: wildlife observation and photography, environmental education and interpretation, fishing, and hunting. A pre-acquisition compatibility determination was also reviewed and completed, and identifies which existing public uses would be allowed to continue on new properties acquired by the Refuge complex. Since releasing the draft CCP/EA, we have also distributed compatibility determinations for trapping and waterfowl hunting for a public review period. All comments were considered and utilized in the revision. These new compatibility determinations are now final and included in Appendix D.

Additional compatibility determinations will be developed when appropriate new uses are proposed. Compatibility determinations will be re-evaluated by the Refuge Manager when conditions under which the use is permitted change significantly; when there is significant new information on effects of the use; or at least every 10 years for non-priority public uses. Priority public use compatibility determinations will be re-evaluated under the conditions noted above, or at least every 15 years with revision of the CCP. Additional detail on the compatibility determination process is in Parts 25, 26, and 29 of Title 50 of the Code of Federal Regulations, effective November 17, 2000.

Additional NEPA Analysis

The National Environmental Policy Act (NEPA) requires a site-specific analysis of impacts for all federal actions. These impacts are to be disclosed in either an EA or Environmental Impact Statement (EIS).

Most of the actions and associated impacts in this plan were described in enough detail in the draft CCP/EA to comply with NEPA, and will not require additional environmental analysis. Although this is not an all-inclusive list, the following programs are examples that fall into this category: protecting piping plover, restoring area-defined grasslands and wetlands, implementing priority wildlife-dependent public use programs (except deer hunting), acquiring land, and controlling invasive plants.

Other actions are not described in enough detail to comply with the site-specific analysis requirements of NEPA. Examples of actions that will require a separate EA include: construction of a new visitor center and headquarters, new deer hunting opportunities, and future habitat restoration projects not fully developed or delineated in this document. Monitoring, evaluation, and research can generally be increased without additional NEPA analysis.

Plan Amendment and Revision

Periodic review of the CCP will be required to ensure that objectives are being met and management actions are being implemented. Ongoing monitoring and evaluation will be an important part of this process. Monitoring results or new information may indicate the need to change our strategies.

The Service's planning policy (FWS Manual, Part 602, Chapters 1, 3, and 4) states that CCPs should be reviewed at least annually to decide if they require any revisions (Chapter 3, part 3.4 (8)). Revisions will be necessary if significant new information becomes available, ecological conditions change, major refuge expansions occur, or when we identify the need to do so during a program review. At a minimum, CCPs will be fully revised every 15 years. We will modify the CCP documents and associated management activities as needed, following the procedures outlined in Service policy and NEPA requirements. Minor revisions that meet the criteria for categorical exclusions (550 FW 3.3C) will only require an Environmental Action Statement.

www.ingramcontent.com/pod-product-compliance
Lightning Source LLC
Chambersburg PA
CBHW080524290526
45790CB00006B/2307